I Drank the Water Everywhere

CHARLES N. BARNARD

I Drank the Water Everywhere

DODD, MEAD & COMPANY · NEW YORK

ACKNOWLEDGMENTS

Because much of this material of mine has appeared before, though in a somewhat different form, I should like to thank *Signature, Physician's World, The New York Times,* and *Global Courier* of Japan Air Lines for their generous cooperation.

Library of Congress Cataloging in Publication Data

Barnard, Charles N
   I drank the water everywhere.

     1. Voyages and travels—1951–   I. Title.
G464.B345   910'.4   75–29212
ISBN 0–396–07211–9

FOR KAREN, WHO WAS ALWAYS THERE

Contents

I Drank the Water Everywhere

CHAPTER 1
Introduction

SOMEONE ASKED me, what does it mean—"I drank the water everywhere?" I said it wasn't intended to boast that I'd been everywhere, nor was it to suggest a foolhardy disregard for typhoid. It simply means, what the hell, let's go have some fun, let's see this old world while we can, and let's not just pick the soft, sunny spots or the people we think we'd like. Let's go wherever the road turns and see what adventures travel will lead us to.

This book, then, is an account of some things we saw and did in the last few years, things that just happened to happen to an itinerant magazine writer and his young wife on their way to assignments around the world. It is not intended to make any profound statements about that world or any parts of it. It is not even intended to promote travel. It has none of what is usually called "service value." It will not show you how to do anything for $5 or $10 a day, it will recommend no particular hotel or airline, it won't help you beat inflation, it won't tell you where best to shop and it will not serve as a restaurant guide, historical guide or any sort of guide to any place.

My book is just an invitation to come along with us and see what we saw.

When the idea of putting some of my magazine pieces together was first conceived, I thought I would surely write a grand opening chapter, one which would express all my feelings about travel, all my love of far places—a paean, if you will, to all the adventurous journeys of my life. Well, I have found that easier said than done. The truth is, I am simply in love with travel, heels over head; no excuses, no apologies, and love is a very difficult emotion to describe rationally. How can I tell you what I feel when I see Hong Kong? Or what escapist excitement tingles my brain each time I step up to an airline counter, lay my ticket and passport down and say, "I'm on your 7 o'clock to Kuala Lumpur." Bags packed, cameras ready, reservations made, a long flight ahead . . .

For me, there have been two sorts of pleasure in all this—to travel and to *have* traveled. The first is activist, full of excitement and sometimes anxiety, my senses curiously sharpened by not quite enough sleep, the euphoria of being exhausted in a good cause. The second pleasure, to *have* traveled, is contemplative and mellow, it is money in the memory bank, it is always to be as young as I was in 1959, it is to close my eyes and see the Serengeti again the way it looked that first time.

I think I am about at mid-point now, both traveler and traveled. It's a little like that moment when you are quite sure of your opinion of a bottle of wine or a piece of beef. You could be wrong, but you're pretty sure you're not. I've traveled enough to want to see more; I've also traveled enough to know the meaning of home.

There's an old cliché which says travel is broadening. I never found out what that means. Perhaps there are travelers whose understanding of world trade or emerging nations or historic ethnic hostilities has been improved by being involved first hand. That kind of travel is, I suppose, like a short course in economics or sociology. Then there are the travelers who are culture freaks. For them, the Rennaissance is in Florence and Dvorak is in Prague and the Mona Lisa is in the Louvre and to partake of these cultural treasures, one must go, one must be present. So must the scientists who are drawn overseas by medical research in Stockholm, archaeology in the Great Rift Valley or marine biology on the Great Barrier Reef. Their travels, like those of businessmen, are just long commutes from home to work.

For me, travel is only escape and adventure. Call it broadening hedonism. An experience of the senses and the emotions. A feeling of being freed, lines cast off and the balloon rising; a feeling of not knowing what I will find or how things will turn out.

Would the shell fish at Lau Fau Shan poison me? That concern was erased in the excitement of being in the tiny Chinese fishing village and seeing its famous oysters, big as size-10 shoes.

Would the Palestinian guerrillas shoot at my Israeli Army jeep along the Lebanese border? Would it have been any fun being there if there wasn't a chance?

Would the elevator cable break as I went down 5000 feet into the gold mine on Fiji? If it did, I would sure miss a good party back in Suva tonight.

Taking the risks, even exaggerating them, was part of the fun of being there for me, a self-styled adventurer in a world all too short of adventure.

Some of my thrill in traveling is in movement, per se. A big Boeing jet under full power at take off still gives me goosebumps. The 125-mph Japanese bullet trains or the elegant Mistral from Paris to Nice are magic carpets of escape. Likewise, the old ferry from Macau, the cable car up Mt. Blanc, a sailing caique between any two Greek islands, the funicular through the Jungfrau tunnel, a police van in the Australian outback, a Swiss lake steamer to Interlaken, an air-cushion train in France, a rickshaw in Hong Kong, a hydrofoil to the pearl farms of Toba, a helicopter to Yokoi's cave on Guam, a camel at the pyramids, a surfboard at Waikiki, a Land Rover in Kenya—or George Greenfield's old Alvis, driving across Dartmoor at dusk.

Going somewhere. Movin' on. Trying to put my arms around the world.

Sometimes, of course, it has been pretty awful. When somebody else's war forces an unscheduled arrival in a city you didn't intend to visit and when the hotel is a horror and some native steals your handbaggage, even the most enthusiastic traveler, even the professional, can despair.

There is probably a form of reciprocity in the fact that if you love movement, you can be emotionally demolished by the lack of it. If getting on a boat to go somewhere is fun, the boat which doesn't arrive, leaving you stranded on an island, is one of those bad breaks which, as a veteran traveler, you are supposed to accept with philosophic calm, but which nevertheless squeezes your gizard with anger and frustration.

Because the breaks in travel can go either way, certain airports can be places of either joyous or miserable memory. Fog and other mechanical misfortunes kept me waiting in total boredom for 14 hours at Orly one winter day and I've never liked the place since. But my first ride in a Boeing 747 was on Japan Air Lines from Honolulu to Tokyo—a happy, flower-decked, champagne-bubbly departure that Karen and I will remember always.

Let's see then, where was I? Trying to explain the mystique of travel. Trying to explain what brightens my eye and quickens my breath. I was going to say it all in a big-bang opening that would explain perfectly. Perhaps it would be better just to tell a short story of an encounter I had once with another traveler.

◆   ◆   ◆

The Masai warrior was walking easily toward me in the sunlight, his bare feet making puffs of dust in the road, his spear held at the exact vertical, mud in his hair and a rust colored toga tied at one shoulder. I had never seen him before, but in another sense I had known him since I was a boy reading *National Geographic* and the books of Martin Johnson. Now the meeting was more exciting than an encounter with a celebrity. It was made more so because my first Masai and I were at the center of Africa's greatest amphitheatre, the largest volcanic crater in the world, Ngorongoro. To me, the name sounds like the roll of black fingers on a skin-head drum: *en-go-ro-go-ro, en-go-ro-go-ro*.

It is easy enough to get to Africa these days. The TWA jet had taken me from New York to Athens to Kenya in swift stages and there was even a new Hilton in Nairobi where the lobby was busy at all hours with travelers who had come to see East Africa's animals "before the poachers and the pollution kills them all," someone said. As for me, I would skip the nearby game parks with all their zebra-striped mini-buses and head for the Serengeti—and the giant crater.

There's a pleasant lodge on the rim, a sort of base camp decorated with old elephant skulls. It affords a great panoramic view of Ngorongoro, like looking at a map before making a journey. In the early morning, fog spills 2000 feet down into the bowl from the surrounding plain like a slow-motion waterfall and you begin to have a measure of how big the big volcanos were when earth was formed in fire and eruption.

"The floor is 102 square miles in area," a guide tells you as you eat pancakes and sausages and look out the lodge windows at the crater. "It's 12 miles across at the rim . . ."

On the way down, the Land Rover lurches and slides in what must be mechanical pain as it negotiates the boulder-strewn road from the edge of the plain into the giant depression. Then, suddenly, I was there, on the bottom, no longer a visitor looking down at the animals of Creation, but now a fellow passenger in an Ark where 50,000 wild things live.

The Masai did not step from the road to let us pass, but kept to his true course as we swung off and stopped. I watched him with fascination: a young man who, I knew, drinks blood, lives in a dung house, kills lions with a spear, scorns civilization and does not say *Jambo* when he meets strangers. I knew I would remember him always, remember him *and* me, just as we were at this moment, both of us at the bottom of earth's own cauldron.

Both of us on the same journey.

CHAPTER 2
Micronesia: Then and Now

THE WIND PRESSED across Truk lagoon out of a dark sky, blowing in all the way from the Marshalls, making the sea rise in the passes between the green islands. We were crossing between Feffen and Dublon in a clout-nailed plywood boat and the man had both Evinrudes churning to keep the small craft steady. When the conical peak of deserted Dublon loomed close on our right, I wondered if he remembered when this was a fortress of the Japanese.

"What did they have up there?" I asked, pointing.

The boatman was a chunky, dark man, a Micronesian in a flowered shirt, khaki pants and rubber zoris. Was he old enough? Had he been here 28 years ago when Truk lagoon was the mightiest naval base in the western Pacific and Dublon Island was its reinforced concrete heart?

He looked at the peak. "You know what they had up there?" he shouted above the noise of the motors. "A big siren, the biggest siren, and you could hear it all over. When American planes came, the Japanese would start the siren and everyone would run."

American planes eventually sank more than 60 Japanese ships at Truk and turned the lagoon into what scuba divers now call an underwater museum. Some of the bombers had come from Kwajalein. I remember because I was there when the pilots came back and talked about impregnable Truk where whole islands had been leveled to make airstrips—a place that was going to make the war last longer for all of us.

"You were here?"

He pointed at the next island. "On Feffen," he said. "They had their best shooters on Feffen." He made a pistol at the sky with his fingers. "Boom, boom, boom. They could hit planes even at night."

I wanted him to remember these things because that is why I had come back to the Pacific—to see what was left of my old war, to look for the traces of where we had been and what we had done, to find out whether time, and now jet planes and tourism, had changed everything.

Boatman lighted a Winston cigarette skillfully against the wind and tugged the grips of the outboards onto a new course toward the dock of the $2 million Continental Hotel. It has 56 rooms and was built in 1970 on the site of an old Japanese seaplane ramp. Business was slow at Truk in those days, but it's picking up now. They have a happy hour every night in the bar and visiting tank divers and their girl friends from California and Hawaii sit around and talk about Truk's sunken ships by name, while Trukese natives with flowers in their hair and crumpled American dollars in their fists, sit quietly by themselves and drink beer from cans.

◆ ◆ ◆

Micronesia is a name which geographers have given to 2100 small islands spread over 3 million square miles of the Pacific. It is a place where Americans and Japanese fought many of the cruelest battles of World War II: Kwajalein, Truk, Saipan, Pelelieu. Indeed, the war and its relics still haunt the area like a rusty memorial. There is hardly an island which does not figuratively beckon today's visitor with a, *"Psst! Want to see an old Japanese gun?"* Even where demolition experts and scrap dealers have dug up and carted off most of the old hardware, there is enough left to kindle the imagination and provide tour guides with expert advice for tourist photographers: "You'll get your best picture of that tank after 4 P.M."

In all this watery empire, larger in size than the U.S., there are only 700 square miles of dry land and perhaps 100 inhabited islands. On these live 100,000 native people. Their average age is about 17, their average income is only a few hundred dollars a year and their social plight is something that everybody talks about but nobody seems to know how to remedy. Tens of thousands of Micronesians whose parents survived the war now exist in ghetto squalor in district centers; only a minority still live as they did a century ago on outlying islands. Throughout Micronesia, the wreckage of war stands side by side with the pollution of peace—rusting, derelict cars everywhere, non-existent sanitation, juvenile delinquency, mounting nutritional problems, declining exports and food production. It is as if a century of colonial domination (Spanish, German, Japanese and now the American-administered United Nations Trust Territory) had finally reduced a once proud and independent people to the ultimate apathy of drinking Milwaukee beer and listening to Nashville music.

John Sablan, District Administrator of Truk, says, "Our coconuts are heavy on the trees and the price of copra (dried coconut) is high, but no one wants to harvest the crop. Our fish are still in the sea, but now it is the Japanese who come and catch them and sell them back to us in cans."

That the people of these islands will ever have the incentive to live their lives in dignity is a result that the strategies of national power may never permit. By an accident of geography, the Micronesian homeland seems destined always to be somebody's battleground or somebody's fortress. In the years since World War II, the U.S. has used its newly conquered Eden as (1) a nuclear testing ground at Bikini and Eniwetok; (2) a missile range at Kwajalein; (3) a nerve gas storage depot at Johnston; (4) a combat B52 base in the Marianas; (5) an ICBM launching site at Wake; (6) a secret CIA training ground on Saipan; and (7) a home port for Polaris submarines at Guam.

And now, in the 1970s, the islands and their people are braced, somewhat apprehensively, for a new invasion: tourism.

◆ ◆ ◆

Evening was coming and they were putting up the movie screen by the beach again, a big piece of canvas between two poles. A few early arrivals moved chairs and sat facing the white rectangle, waiting for the sky to be dark enough for the picture. Overhead, cutting through clouds that were still pink, a big bomber droned toward the airfield at the north end of the island. Beyond the beach, the Pacific pounded the reef with the familiar sound of a long freight.

For an old soldier who had come back, it was all the way it should be; all the pieces were in place: Lt. Bell was up there in the bomber, returning home with his case of beer chilled by the cold of the rear turret. And Sgt. Carr had his half-pound Hersey bar and his home-made chair tilted back just so for the movie. Soon Rock Happy Regula would come in from the reef with his bag of shells, which he would put under the barracks where the ants would eat out the creatures inside.

Then light flickered on the screen and illusion dissolved. It was still the Pacific, but it wasn't my war. The time was now and the island was Guam. The beach and the surf and even the bomber (a B52, not a B29) were there, but the movie was at the Hilton hotel pool and the audience was a generation of young Japanese who had never fought for their lives in Guam's caves, but who come here each week by the thousands on their honeymoons.

Guam isn't Micronesia, but it is the gateway to the area, a poor, dusty, tin-roof sort of *barrio* which, because it is U.S. soil, likes to say it is "where America's day begins." In 1941, after Pearl Harbor, America's day ended on Guam and the island fell to the Japanese. It was recaptured 3½ years later in savage battles. During the occupation, Guamanians learned to hate the Japanese. Now, ironically, Guam plays obliging host to the children of the old enemy; the island has become a low-cost Japanese vacation paradise only 3½ air hours south of teeming Tokyo. The guests come on an endless packaged tour, arriving via Japan Air Lines and Pan Am jumbo jets—150,000 a year now, 250,000 next year, half a million soon? The polite young men with their cameras and their little brides in bright muu muus have become the biggest fact of life on the island. They are 90 percent of Guam's tourists. The money they spend has built an industry of high-rise hotels, restaurants, gift shops, golf courses and sightseeing tours. It is an industry which many expect to spread to other islands of Micronesia.

Menus on Guam are written in English and Japanese, raw fish and cold rice are available everywhere for breakfast, tables are set as a matter of course with chop sticks and bottles of soy sauce, entertainers sing *Bali Hai* in Japanese and Chief Kawana, a full-blooded Maori from New Zealand who does a lively Polynesian show at the Hilton, tells Japanese jokes. Japanese cars outsell American ones, Japanese investment money builds hotels, resorts and golf courses, and, until a few irate locals complained, some hotels even flew the Japanese flag. There is a wry joke which says Guam really belongs to Japan now because the last survivor of World War II to give up on the island was a Japanese army sergeant named Yokoi who hid out in a cave for 28 years before surrendering in 1972. (A year later there were still reports of Japanese "stragglers" thought to be hiding out in the island's rugged interior.)

Traces of my old war may linger on Guam, but many of the island businessmen want it over with now. They say the young Japanese who are so important to Guam's future don't care about Yokoi's cave or the rusty tanks their fathers died in; they say the future is in new scuba dive shops, motorcycle rentals, tennis courts and supper clubs. But that is tomorrow; today is still an in-between time, a time when old things can still be seen and touched and remembered, a twilight before they close the books on those days.

For example, if you follow a dirt road past a lot of junk cars, you can still find the war dog cemetary on Guam. It's covered with weeds now, but some of the markers are legible. "Silver" was a PFC. And near the Okura Hotel, at a place called Gun Beach, an old Japanese howitzer pokes out from a cave full of beer cans and contraceptives. And at the end of another dirt road, with no sign to mark it, a memorial to Japanese war dead stands in tall grass. It was built with private funds on private property, cast in concrete to resemble hands in prayer. Lizards dart about on its stark white surface and the remains of Buddhist food offerings rot on its altar.

"Sometimes Japanese visitors ask us why the standard island bus tours don't come here," a guide says. "We tell them it isn't really an official memorial, that there is no public road anyway. The thing should really be torn down. Who cares about this now?"

♦ ♦ ♦

"I've come a long way to see you," I said to the man who walked toward me out of the dim clutter of the general store on Ponape. There was no recognition on his face, just puzzlement.

"I came here first on the destroyer, the day the Japanese surrendered," I said. "We found you and your family in the jungle. Your daughter came down the path carrying an American flag your wife had made by hand."

A smile that said yes spread across his face. He didn't know who I was, but he knew now that I must be one of the Americans who had come that day to free him from 4½ years of imprisonment.

"We thought you would never come," he said quietly in German-accented English. We stood looking at each other, remembering the time and gauging what changes a quarter century had made in our flesh.

"I wrote a story about you for the newspapers," I said.

"Yes. We still have it in a scrapbook. Were you the one who wrote it?"

"I've come to write another story."

A woman wearing a blue dress came up behind the counter where we were talking. She looked at me curiously.

"This is my daughter Yvette," he said. She was the child who had carried the flag.

That night, at a big friendly house in a clearing in the jungle, I met Yvette's children. They sat quietly while Grandpa and the man from America remembered things about an old war.

Carlos Etscheit is in his seventies now. He is Belgian. He has lived on Ponape all his life, trading in copra, making soap, running a store and doing what he calls an import-export business. He says he will never leave this island that has been both

---

his home and his prison, that he will die here and be buried next to his wife. He goes to Europe occasionally, but hurries home because the pace of London or Paris is too much. It is easier for him to travel now because Ponape has an airstrip which a Japanese company built a few years ago and several times a week an Air Micronesia jet whistles in to deliver a few tourists and the mail. There are a couple of hotels on Ponape already and there is talk of others. But the island is more primitive now than when it was Japanese.

"There were 20,000 of them here during the war," Carlos Etscheit said. "It was a prosperous place. I had many Japanese friends. They imprisoned me only because I was Belgian and Belgium was at war with Japan.

"Now they say that American tourism is coming, but I don't know. Why would anyone want to come here? There is nothing to see but the old ruins of Nanmatol." The rain fell heavily outside the house as we talked and beyond the dark windows there was nothing but mystery.

"It's a strange, beautiful place," I said. "Perhaps people who want to get away from everything will come here."

Finally, when it was late, there was a let-up in the rain and it seemed a good time to go. We closed the old picture books then.

"I'm glad you came," he said. "Sometimes these little ones don't believe me when I tell them what happened."

When we said goodbye, I knew I would not see him again. One only expects to get to Ponape once or twice.

◆ ◆ ◆

"Air Mike," as the airline is called, is the glue that holds scattered Micronesia together. It is a division of Continental Airlines in the U.S. Since it began service in 1968, Air Mike has become as much a part of the island scene as palm trees and

brown-skinned people. Its two wholly owned Continental hotels—one in Koror (Palau), the other in Truk—are the best
tourist facilities in the Territory. Its two 727 jets and one old
DC6B are fitted to carry passengers (economy class only) and
cargo and they workhorse their way over thousands of route
miles a day, landing like great birds on short coral strips and
shattering the lazy tranquility of tiny islands with the thunder
of technology. The planes are almost always full and reservations from island to island (usually on an every-other-day
schedule) are a must. Passengers may be betel nut-chewing
natives, officials of the Trust Territory government, scuba divers, medical specialists, military personnel, American tourists,
even some weekend swingers trying to get away from the "pres-
sures" of Kwajalein for some snorkeling at Majuro, less than
an hour away.

People who fly the airline say they feel more like participants
in a common adventure than commercial passengers. They
greet stewardesses and captains alike as old friends and insist
that without Air Mike, the Trust Territory just wouldn't work.

Certainly for any traveler who has been hung up for two or
three rain-soaked days on any one of the islands, the arrival of
the big red, white and gold airplane at the local thatch-roof
airport terminal can seem like a reprieve from prison. In that
sense, today isn't much different from when the planes were
C54s and there was a war on.

◆ ◆ ◆

On Kwajalein, we used to go down to the airstrip in the
evening to see the looks on the faces of replacements coming in
on flights from Hawaii. It was a cruel sport, but, like hanging
around the drugstore, it was something to do in a social
vacuum. Somehow, it gave us long-timers a feeling of faith in
ourselves because we had survived in such a place—a place that

brought looks of shock to newcomers' faces.

"Hey, look at that one! He don't believe this place! Welcome to The Rock, short-timer!" Everyone who ever came to Kwaj remembers the moment. It was like arriving at Devil's Island and being sized up by the old cons.

But when the C54s turned around and lifted off and headed back toward Waikiki where the whisky was (and the girls), everyone, even the old cons, prayed for some excuse to be aboard. Malaria. Section Eight. Treason. Anything would do. We used to watch the departing planes until they were specks, then scuff off to the outdoor movie at the Richardson Theatre. In the audience, sitting on palm logs, you could pick out the new arrivals easy enough. Their clothes weren't bleached yet and their eyes weren't bloodshot and they didn't yet know that the only women on the island were the ones up there on that screen.

◆ ◆ ◆

They have women of all ages on Kwaj today, and they still have a Richardson Theatre, but for an old soldier returning to the Rock, everything seems to be in the wrong place. The one-time Devil's Island has become Suburbia, USA, an island totally transformed by money and technology to make a home for thousands of Americans and their families—the people who send Nike Zeus anti-missile missiles up to intercept ICBMs fired across the Pacific from California.

"We've added 40 acres to the island," a man told me as we drove through neatly manicured neighborhoods of Florida-style houses. I saw a store called Macy's West. There was a nine-hole golf course and tennis courts and kids rode the streets on chopper-style bikes under the shade of coconut palms.

"When I was here, we had one tree," I reminisced. "It was about six feet tall and had three branches. We took pictures of it to prove that the island could really support life."

"What did you do when you were here?"

"Oh, I wrote about the war and I wrote a column for the island newspaper. It was called the Hour Glass."

"Funny you should mention that," the man said. "We just finished throwing out a lot of old files of that paper. It was mimeographed, wasn't it?"

"Yes," I said, "it was." I didn't tell him that I sometimes also turned the mimeo machine crank.

The military won't trust you to pay a long visit to Kwaj these days, not even if you're one of the island's original old cons. Although it is one of the Marshalls and therefore part of the Trust Territory of Micronesia, the place is off-limits to tourists. Air Mike stops there only long enough to take fuel. In fact, so independent is the slick, scientific new Kwajalein that it ignores the International Dateline and observes the same calendar day as Vandenberg AFB. After all, you couldn't launch a missile one day and intercept it the day before, now could you?

When I climbed onto Air Mike to leave Kwaj, I didn't look back with nostalgia. They'd made a nice place out of my old Rock indeed, but I think I liked it better before Dr. Strangelove added the 40 acres and the golf course.

◆ ◆ ◆

If the military still plays a major role in many parts of Micronesia, there are also places where neither the ghosts of World War II nor the spectre of World War III seem to intrude on virgin nature. Palau is a remarkable example. You can get there in an hour from Guam and just before you land, the pilot will probably get on the intercom and tell his passengers that Jacques Cousteau calls this one of the five greatest diving spots in the world, so clear is the water. Below, you will see hundreds of small islands which, like hovercraft, seem to float upon, yet not quite touch, the surface of the sea. In shape, the Rock Islands of Palau have been likened to haystacks, soldier's helmets or toadstools. Their lush green vegetation looks as carefully sculpted as the hedges of Versailles, yet no hand has ever touched them. What is the mystery of this flotilla of islands lying perpetually at anchor? Why are there no beaches where they meet the water? Why no signs of life?

"The only way to understand them is by boat," Hank Hickox told me. "We'll have one ready for you in the morning." Hickox is manager of the Continental Hotel on Koror, principal island of the Palau group. With his Hawaii-born wife, Johnna, he struggles with the problems of running a first-class American hotel in an impoverished boondocks community of 5000 Micronesians. To provide a safe haven for international guests, the Continental generates its own electricity, has its own independent water supply, and, because there is no milk in Micronesia, is thinking of getting its own cow.

"You might find this hard to believe in a Pacific paradise," says Hickox, "but my main worry here is getting enough to eat: fresh fruit, vegetables, fish, meat. Next year I think we'll try planting our own garden."

When Koror was Japanese, it supported a population of 30,000 and exported foodstuffs all over the western Pacific. Today there is no agriculture on Koror, but there are supermarkets on the unpaved main street. The shelves are stocked, for the most part, with food from Japan.

The boat was ready the next morning. As we moved out, rain storms on the horizon looked as flat and gray as sheets of slate. They moved behind the islands like scenery in an amphitheatre, altering what we saw with optical tricks. Were the Rock Islands black or green? Did they float like a mirage over a silvery desert or did they rise, like the mushroom cloud of Bikini, on a root column of their own? We watched the distant storms, but cleaved sunny waters, aiming for narrow channels between the islands, speeding along shorelines of solid limestone undercut by the sea to form a continuous cave. Overhanging this cave was a jungle without earth, an inpenetrable interlocking of primeval growth rooted like a hanging garden into a base of pocked and tortured stone.

There is as yet no scientific explanation for the Rock Islands. That they were formed, like coral, by the skeletal remains of lime-secreting creatures is probable. That they were undercut by some marine organism with an appetite for limestone has been suggested. No one knows. If they were not hidden away in the remote western Pacific, they would surely be as famous a tourist attraction as the Petrified Forest or Carlsbad Cavern.

About 15 miles south of Koror, we found a small beach and ate some lunch and explored a reef that swarmed with neon bright fish. Later the rain swept over us with the power of a 10-minute car wash. Then we headed home, looking into great caves along the way. Even the Rock Islands have a few old Japanese guns still pointing at the empty sea.

◆　◆　◆

Where did my war turn in the Pacific? At Tarawa or Kwaj? Pelelieu or Iwo? Every island makes a claim, but in the Marianas the tour guides say Japan was really finished when the big bombers started lifting off the airfields at Saipan and Tinian. Flying in from Guam, you can see those famous old strips, hemmed in with wild growth now, yet still defiantly and timelessly straight.

It is probably symbolic of Micronesia's destiny that on Tinian the U.S. military has plans to reactivate the airbase that launched the *Enola Gay* and the atomic age, while on Saipan one of the old 9000-foot B29 runways is being converted into a new commercial airfield for jumbo jets. Guns and tourism. Nowhere are they closer than on Saipan.

They say you can see the 14-mile island in three or four hours by car, but not if you've been here before, not if you're old enough to believe in ghosts. Japanese honeymooners come on day trips from Guam and busses take them to places like Hari Kiri Gulch or Suicide Cliff where, in the final days of the war, their ancestors plunged to ritual deaths by the thousands rather than accept American conquest. Today's young tourists take pictures, look over the precipice, then stroll back to the bus— where the guide puts contemporary Japanese music in the tape deck. He probably won't tell them all he knows about this place; that whole families said goodbye to one another here, that children pushed children over the 800-foot cliff, youngest first, until there was none left but the eldest for the parents to kill before jumping themselves.

On all the islands of Micronesia, but particularly on Saipan, the lost dead of the war have brought about a melancholy rite: the gathering of the bones of unknown soldiers by religious and military delegations from Japan. Hotel keepers call these groups "memorial guests." They are good customers; they usually stay a month or more. From the rocks below Suicide Cliff to the dark, silty interiors of dead ships and submarines on the bottom of Truk lagoon, the reverent bone hunters have retrieved the remains of their loved ones.

Traditionally, after the bones are gathered, a funeral pyre is built of logs, a Rising Sun flag is draped over the top and an ancient dirge is sung as flames bring a proper rest at last to victims of the old war.

There is a sadness about Saipan, not only because so many thousands died here, but because it was a place of noble ambitions which was shattered and never put together again. For 30 years it had been a pretty green island with soaring highlands where 30,000 Japanese ran a tight colonial ship, raising sugar cane, pork, bananas and vegetables. Indeed, the island was part of something called the Greater East Asia Co-Prosperity Sphere. After December 7, 1941, that became an ugly phrase. From Saipan, sugar and molasses and alcohol went to the home islands. Unfortunately, guns and tanks and fighter planes came back.

Even after the holocaust of war, there are traces of the old agricultural regime that survive on the island today: a great bronze statue of Haruji Matsue, still curiously intact, stands with inappropriate dignity in what was once a small green park. He was Saipan's sugar king, father of its economy, educated in the U.S. There is a clean bullet hole through his neck. And there are living survivors: rows of graceful Norfolk pines planted as windbreaks long ago on the lagoon beach, their tough roots still holding deep in the fine white sand; and African snails, an obscene sort of pest, once imported as pig feed, now out of control and eating their way through the island like an armored invasion.

"If the snails would only eat all the *tangan tangan* and die from it!" is the prayer of many a Saipanese as he looks at the jungle of brushy green that now covers 90 percent of the island. This thriving, weedy growth was seeded from the air by the U.S. to cover Saipan's shell-torn, denuded landscape. It has become an unwanted mantle that kills everything in its path, a triumph of quick technocracy, but a tragedy for Saipan.

There are two good hotels on the island today and more coming, including a new member of the Continental chain. All face the old invasion beaches and wait for the new invasion of tourism. Saipan, they say, is the place where it's really going to happen: night clubs, golf driving ranges, yachting, scuba diving, helicopter tours—it will all be here. Both Pan Am and Continental are vying for the rights to fly the customers in direct from Tokyo; Japan Air Lines already owns the route.

"It will change us completely," says a Saipanese member of the Trust Territory government. "And it may ruin us."

An old soldier asks if the war memorials, already rusted and nibbled away by souvenir hunters, will be restored for the new waves of tourists. Aren't they important?

"The war stuff is just for the short term," says a tourism specialist with the Trust Territory Department of Development. "According to our studies, interest in this factor of our present tourist package will decline rapidly in the coming years. It brings in a few dollars now, but the people who are interested have a high average age and will soon be gone. Then who will care?"

The man was right, of course. Old soldiers may never die, but their wars *do* fade away.

CHAPTER 3
A Sentimental Harvest

SIDE TRIPS can be some of the special joys of travel—
trips-within-trips which become short, memorable adventures:
by hydrofoil from Hong Kong to Macau for an evening of
roulette; by car from London to the Cotswolds for a weekend
with friends; by train from Tokyo to Nikko to visit the temples;
from Rome to Tivoli for a day with the Emperor Hadrian; and,
by all means, from Paris to the Champagne country at harvest
time.

I have particular reasons for remembering Champagne. I realize
they have probably given the place a special meaning for me. But
it is a beautiful region all the same and even if your trip there is
not a sentimental journey, I think it should be a happy one.

Tourists in Paris have many options for side trips: Versailles,
the cathedral at Chartres, Fontainebleau, the chateaux of the
Loire. They are all famous and beautiful, bathed in floodlight
by night, surrounded by souvenir shops, their parking areas

overflowing with busses, their paths well worn by millions of visitors. They are "sights," as in "seeing the sights," things to be looked at. Buy your ticket and enter. But sights are often dead things, monuments of stone. Castles can be cold and cathedrals aloof. For those who want what the French call *joie de vivre;* the Champagne district in the fall is a warm, back-to-nature experience that can linger in memory like a childhood trip to grandfather's farm.

I wanted Karen to see this. I wanted her to see everything I had seen before, anything from that earlier life that I had liked and remembered and didn't want to lose. Some things would never be recovered, perhaps, but there was still time for others; there were places and feelings that could be recaptured and put back in their proper order.

"You've never seen anything like it," I said as we were arranging for the car. "Grape vines from horizon to horizon." I always feel an excitement about starting a journey to a new place, but returning to a familiar one can be full of affection—especially if you have someone to show it to.

"But you've seen it all before," young Karen said as if she meant that I had peeked.

"Never mind, it's your turn," I told her, hoping it would be perfect, hoping it would all be as I remembered it.

The *vendange,* as the French call their harvest, is a happy time in this small region which produces the festive, bubbly wine. Bacchus seems present in every vineyard and the country-side vibrates with the sounds of tractors and tank trucks laboring up hills loaded with grapes or juice. An event, a rite of nature, is taking place and it will happen here every year whether tourists come or not. Of course, they do come, by the thousands; a visit to Champagne is a favorite fall holiday for the French. They like to be there when the Pinot Noir and Char-

donnay grapes ripen and begin their trip from the sunny hillsides to the cool limestone caves underground.

So do I. My first visit was 15 years ago, a happy time for me, soon
to end. The world changed after that and so did I, but the vines
know nothing about change or time. They will always be there,
with roots which reach 30 feet into the limestone. Others may own
this precious land which is worth $50,000 an acre, but it is the vines
which hold it, like an army of occupation that will not go away.

Although the harvest is a performance played out by many
actors and extras on a great stage, there is no price of admission.
If you go there, only 90 miles from Paris, you simply become
a part of the festivities, as much as the man in blue coveralls
with the basket of grapes balanced on his shoulder. You say
bonjour and he will reply whether he knows you or not. You
share the spirit of this time and place.

The road from Paris to Champagne is Route Nationale 3,
well-marked and easy to follow. If you leave the city early, you
can be in the heart of the district, the small city of Epernay, for
lunch. For the first 30 miles out of Paris, the traffic is heavy and
the scenery disappointing, but then the country opens and the
road begins to look like a French road is supposed to look:
string straight and poplar-lined for miles, passing through
farmland and small towns. This is war's old invasion route; the
way the armies have always come, the way to Soissons and
Verdun, to Sedan and Chateau Thierry. There are military
memorials along the way which stand as monuments to old
follies, final resting places for other generations of Americans
who thought they too would secure peace with honor. If you
see a direction sign to one of the World War I cemeteries, it is
worthy of a few minutes detour to admire the serene perfection

with which they are still maintained, more than half a century after the white marble crosses were first put in place, row upon sad row.

I didn't know whether she would care about this or not, whether it was just a thing old soldiers understand but can never explain to a younger woman, not even to this one who could always read my mind. There's nothing jolly about so many sleeping ghosts; a visit to a cemetery wasn't the harvest festival I'd promised, I knew.

We walked, hand in hand, on the finely raked gravel paths and marvelled at grass clipped to carpet perfection and bright flowers blooming and tall trees standing at attention. Whoever cared for this formal garden of sorrow was unseen at the moment; we were alone, in step with the joy of being alive. Although no name on any cross had meaning, the accumulated meaning of the place made me thoughtful and thankful.

"It's all surprisingly beautiful," Karen said finally, and then with a squeeze of her hand she added, "But I'm glad you're not here."

"How could I be?" I said, also wanting to change the mood. "This was the wrong war for me. Mine was later."

"I don't remember either of them," Karen answered.

Eastward from Chateau Thierry, the route to Champagne follows the south bank of the Marne, but although Epernay is 30 miles distant, no vineyards are yet visible. At Dormans, however, a traveler can join one of the traditional sightseeing routes of the region by crossing to the north bank of the river and following the well-marked "Champagne Road" for the last 18 miles. This passes through or near five or six small towns and affords the first spectacular views of the Marne valley and its thousands of acres of Champagne grapes. By French law, the famous wine can be made only from the vineyards of this area.

The vines often grow to the edge of the road and in October they are splashed with leaves of autumnal red and gold, the tight bunches of green or indigo grapes heavy with juice. The date for beginning the harvest can vary as much as two weeks from year to year, depending on the weather, but once picking begins, the entire 50,000-acre area swarms with nearly 60,000 migrant *vendangeurs* who, in two or three weeks time, will cut over 13,000 tons of grapes.

The workers come back to this job each year for generations. Sometimes whole families arrive together, often travelling in rusted old busses, their labor contracted for in advance by agents of the champagne companies. For the most part, the pickers come from Lorraine and Pas de Calais where, for 11 months of the year, many work as coal miners. Their annual pilgrimage to the harvest is, to them, a paid vacation, a month of hard work but happy days in the autumn sun.

A champagne grower once told me, "These people come from a sad, gray region. Once summer is over, they seldom see the sky or the sun. They believe that if they come here once a year in October they will live longer." The pickers say it is like "a cure in three parts: a rest cure, a weather cure and a wine cure."

Most growers provide the *vendangeurs,* each man, woman and child, with a litre of ordinary wine a day, feed them well, house them in permanent dormitories or in tent cities (which you may sometimes see from the road) and pay them according to a scale which is negotiated anew each year. In 1973, boys under 17 received $1.25 a day. A *chef d'équipe,* who supervises the work of about 50 pickers, gets $2.50. There has never been a strike against the champagne firms by the migrant workers. Both sides seem to understand that a disruption of the harvest would mean (1) economic ruin for the companies, (2) a spoiled holiday for the workers and (3) a change in life's way that neither side wants.

Seen from a distance, the pickers look like scouting parties for an advancing army, little clusters of men in uniforms of blue, only their heads and shoulders showing above the long, parallel rows of vines, moving slowing along the ridges, carrying small baskets of grapes to bigger baskets, then heaving these up onto the trucks and trailers that rumble along the roads like armor in a battle zone.

We were about to pass one of these vehicles on the narrow road. Seen from the rear, the grapes were piled so high that nothing else was visible, but as we went by we could see the youngsters riding all over the tractor, hanging on, singing, holding up the biggest bunches of grapes for us to see and admire.

"I told you about that, didn't I?" I said to Karen. "Remember I said the kids looked as if they should be in school instead of out working. I still don't know why they're not . . ."

"I thought you knew all about champagne," she said mischievously, so to save face I had to tell her what happens at the end of the harvest, how ritual flowers are tossed on the last cartful of grapes to come in from each vineyard and the companies provide turkey and champagne for a traditional feast called the *cochelet* and then there is a great night of dancing and singing before everyone gets paid and heads for home.

At Cumieres on the Champagne Road, a traveler should bear left up to Hautvillers. Not only is there a fine view of the vineyards from here, but this small hillside village has a special significance to the history of champagne: there, three centuries ago in a Benedictine abbey, the monk Dom Perignon discovered the fermentation process which produces the bubbles in champagne. The abbey and its cellars are gone, but Dom Perignon's grave can be seen in the floor of the 18th Century parish church.

Long before Dom Perignon, grapes flourished in the chalky soil of this region. The Romans cultivated vines here and made wine and so, for a thousand years, did those who came after. The white wine of the area was mediocre, however. Not until the monk discovered what a secondary fermentation could do, did the world begin to appreciate that champagne was something special.

From Hautvillers, take the narrow road which winds through the vineyards and foothills, arriving in a few kilometers at Champillon. Pass through the village and up the hill until, just on the left at a fork in the road, you will find the auberge Royal Champagne.

We were going to meet my old friend Bernard for lunch at the auberge—Bernard, who is now a director of one of the champagne firms and who is so authentically French. In earlier years he had taught me all I needed to know to appear an expert on champagne. Now I wanted Karen to meet him.

As I drove up the hill from Champillon, running late and cursing the rented car, I guessed at the expression that Bernard would try to suppress, the poise with which he would greet his American friend and his new wife. Good old Bernard! In our younger days he would drive from Paris to Reims faster than the fastest train— "Because I can not wait to get back to my beloved vineyards!" he would say, laughing at his own jest and ordering another bottle at the Lyon D'Or bar.

I was glad to see that he looked no older now, leaning his long frame against the bar at the auberge, looking reproachfully at his watch as we came in.

"You are late!" he said, pretending annoyance. "But I see you have a beautiful reason," he added, taking Karen's hand.

Any other introduction seemed hardly necessary. A piece of life had just slipped neatly into place. I was back in Champage at last.

The Royal Champagne is a 17th Century coaching inn with narrow staircases and small doorways and floors that squeak. It is still run like a family business, still kept like a private home.

It has been somewhat modernized in recent years and its new exterior unfortunately disguises the warmth within. There are 14 rooms, some in the old, original building, some in a new wing where each has a private garden and terrace and a sunset view looking down the valley toward Epernay. There are other places where a visitor to the harvest might stay, but none that I know of which is surrounded on four sides by grape vines. Royal Champagne cuisine is rated one star by Michelin, meaning it can be very good, and its cathedral ceiling dining room gets three crossed spoons & forks in red from the famous guide, a code for exceptionally pleasant atmosphere.

They know what Bernard likes at the auberge and he knows what is good on the menu. He ordered a particular vintage of his own firm's champagne with lunch and while the restless bubbles raced straight up through the blonde wine like little strings of beads, we talked about this year's harvest, the important technicalities, how many degrees of sugar and acidity in the grapes and what a wet August had probably done to this lot of wine that we would be drinking in three or four years.

"No matter," I said, "you'll make your usual enormous profit!"

A look of pain crossed Bernard's face. "My old friend is joking!" he said. "Have you forgotten what I taught you? That it takes one and a half kilos of grapes for each bottle of wine? At present prices, that is almost $2 for just the raw material."

"But what else do you need to make champagne?"

Bernard ticked off on his fingers: "Hand labor, 50¢ per bottle. The bottle itself, 25¢. Labels, packing, foil, wire and cork, another 25¢."

"Fine," I said. "You're now up to $3, but on New Year's Eve in a New York hotel you can easily pay ten times that much."

The fingers were raised again. "Yes, but we have not yet added French government taxes, the agent's share, the wholesaler's share, the retailer's share, the U.S. government duty, the shipping costs —and the fact that out of every 100 bottles in our cellars, two will explode from internal pressure and are a loss.

"If we make 35¢ a bottle we are lucky!" Bernard shrugged a superb Gallic shrug and looked sadly down into his glass. His story reminded me of a farmer I knew in Vermont who was paid 2¢ a quart for his milk when it cost 20 times that much in the store.

There are many hundreds of companies, large and small, which produce champagne, but of these, fewer than 30 are exporters whose brand names are familiar. The biggest firms have facilities for visitors who want to see how champagne is made. In some cases, an appointment should be made in advance, but in a few of the largest firms tours run on schedule every day, even during the busy harvest season. The old, aristocratic champagne families are famous for their hospitality.

Moët & Chandon, on the main street in Epernay, is the General Motors of the business. They produce over 17 million bottles of bubbly a year and have the largest reserves in the world. Altogether in the Epernay region, more than 400 million bottles of champagne are stored in 120 miles of subterranean caves, enough to supply world demand for years.

A visit at Moët or any of the other major firms takes about an hour and usually begins with a history of champagne and the process for making the wine—from picking the grapes through the pressing, fermentation, blending, bottling and aging. Then an escorted walk through some of the cellars to see bottles by the millions sleeping in cool darkness.

Here is where the products of the sunny harvest are turned into cold cash. The caves are the bank vaults of the champagne business where the interest of time is compounded year after year until a bottle of ordinary white wine turns into something which makes everyone laugh gaily and feel good when it is uncorked with a pop.

Laurent-Perrier at Tours sur Marne is a small firm compared to the two or three giants of the business, but its champagne is sold in almost every country around the world and is noted among *cognoscenti* for fine blending and exquisite quality. The company headquarters is old and tranquil with lovely country gardens and the "tour" is more like a visit to a friend's house . than an industrial inspection.

The first time I came here, long ago, we stood around the small fountain in the courtyard where the figure of a little boy urinates continuously and the admonition "NEVER DRINK WATER" is inscribed in French. Our group was amused by this and some people took pictures of the naughty French statue.

The small reception room at Laurent-Perrier has a family feeling with furnishings like a front parlor and a table at the center where they pour complimentary champagne for visitors. Afternoon light shines through the lively glasses and you can hear the rumble of barrels being rolled about in the warehouse nearby or the snorting of tractors pulling loads of new grapes on the small road in front of the gate.

"Nothing has changed," I said to Bernard. "Your little lad out there is still peeing after all these years."

"There is no need to change things here," he replied. "Our business is to keep things the same." He put the back of his fingers against the side of an open bottle on ice to test the chill. The wine rose high in the tulip glasses when he poured it, then subsided with a hiss.

"It's good to be back," I said, lifting the glass.

"Did you see what you wanted to see this time?"

"Yes, I think we did," I said, looking at Karen.

"Yes," she said. "It was just the way he said it would be."

CHAPTER 4
Telephones and Temple Bells

THE YOUNG MAN who came to the door of the Buddhist temple wore a short crewcut, a sober expression and a baseball jacket with *Giants* lettered across the front. In the pale, bluish light of a fluorescent tube in the entryway, he studied us as if there were some mistake. Whoever were these three travelers who, with far more baggage than is carried in Japan, had just been delivered into the quiet, darkened courtyard by a taxi?

The cab driver, already curious about the American couple and the Japanese man who had been his passengers, waited to see the outcome of the negotiations at the door. Perhaps these three would soon be getting back into his car to go somewhere else.

"Are you sure your reservations were at this temple?" the young man asked, speaking Japanese, and the Japanese guest said yes indeed, they were arranged days earlier in Tokyo.

"It's all right anyway," said the young man in the *Giants* jacket. "We have no pilgrims now." Then he picked up one of the big American suitcases and, pausing for us to leave our

33

shoes among the others on the stone floor of the entry, led the way inside. As I slid my socks silently along the centuries-smooth wooden floor of the corridor, I heard the taxi leaving. Now we were really on our own, guests in a monastery atop 3000-foot Mt. Koya. It would be a purifying experience, I had been assured, a retreat from the troubles of the world, from commercialism; an aesthetic if not a religious adventure, one which many devout Japanese hope to experience at least once before they die.

Koyasan. When the place was first mentioned to me, the name meant nothing; I had never heard of it. Nikko, yes. Nara, Kyoto and Toba, of course. But Koyasan? Where was that?

"It is here, this mountain," said my friend with the Japanese National Tourist Office in New York. He was pointing to a spot on the map not far southwest of Kyoto. "It is one of the holiest places in Japan, founded in 816 A.D. by the great saint, Kobo Daishi. There are probably more religious treasures kept there than anywhere else in the country."

I became more interested when I was told that fewer than a hundred non-Japanese visitors a year go through the ritual of spending a night in one of the 54 monasteries which form the religious community at the top of the mountain.

"It is an experience you shouldn't miss," I was told. "Americans almost never do it. The monks will serve you only vegetarian food, and there will be no alcohol—although," my friend added with a wink, "if you ask for some *hannya-to* (devil water) you may be surprised how much like *sake* it tastes!"

"And what about my wife? Can she stay at Koyasan too?" Monks, I knew, sometimes take a dim view of cohabitation on monastery premises. Would Karen be welcome by the Shingon Buddhists?

"A century ago, absolutely not," was the answer in New

York, "but America is not the only place where women are enjoying liberation. Today your wife will be welcome at the monastery. There is even a ladies room . . ."

Indeed, there was also a double bed made up on the *tatami* when we were shown to our room; two pillows, a thin pad on the floor and a large, down-filled quilt overall. It was a spacious room with a sliding paper partition between the sleeping area and what I called the living room. Although there was no furniture in the usual sense, the room contained a large color TV set (which promised to produce a picture when 200 yen was inserted in the pay slot), a telephone (which would produce no dial tone at any price), a kerosene heater with a small glowing window which gave off very little warmth, a fire extinguisher and, at the center of the floor, a short-legged card table covered with an oversized tablecloth which was actually a quilt.

Our Japanese companion, Hideo Hamano, said we should sit at the table now. "To get warm," he added, although I didn't see the connection until I got down on the floor and slipped my stocking feet under the overflow of the quilt. Surprisingly, the space enclosed beneath was a veritable oven thanks to an electric heater fitted to the underside of the table.

"Very cozy," I observed. It was October and the mountain air was cold.

"Old Japanese custom," Hamano said, smiling. "But it wasn't always electric."

The young man who had escorted us to the room returned now to take our orders for dinner. Hamano spoke with him briefly in Japanese. I caught the term *hannya-to*. The young man nodded without expression. In a short time he was back with a helper. They carried three nests of small tables, stacked three high. The tables were already set with plates and bowls containing our food and a *tokkuri* of *sake* each. Hamano explained that the importance of the meal should be judged by the number of tables for each guest. One portable table was standard, a second table was the sign of a superior meal, but a *third* side table was a high compliment. My third table bore my desert, two small "raviolis" (I called them) filled with sweetish red bean jam.

The three-table system unfortunately required us to abandon the comfort of the electric footwarmer and there was nothing about *shojin ryori* (vegetarian) cooking which proved very hearty. Fried chrysanthemum leaves are tasty but delicate. The effects of the kerosene heater notwithstanding, I didn't think there could be much difference between the room temperature and the wintery air outside. I remembered my own Puritan New England origins and wondered if the chill might be a calculated part of the purification process for which Koyasan was famous.

Then the telephone rang. The sound was a shock, coming from what had seemed a dead instrument. Also, after a 14-mile ascent of the mountain on a road with endless hairpin curves, I thought we had surely left the world of communications behind. We looked at each other, mystified. A phone call *here?* Hamano answered and listened.

"Your bath is ready," he announced. "One of the monks just said so."

It was getting late and our friend excused himself to retire. Karen and I changed into kimonos which were provided and made our way along unlighted, open air porches, looking for the bath. My feet kept coming out of the tiny slippers. There was no person in sight, but in the central part of the monastery we heard voices behind partitions and smelled cooking. I wondered if it were the monks. I had not seen one yet, but I wanted to. What is a monastery, after all, without monks?

We found the bath behind a pair of glass doors, a modern tiled pool in a warm, steamy room. Someone had made everything ready for us. The bath was not private, but inasmuch as Karen and I seemed to be the only guests, we felt no particular concern about others joining us in our nakedness. We soaped and showered first, then lowered our bodies into the scorching whirlpool of the "tub." Koyasan may be mysterious, even contradictory, I thought, but it was beginning to feel more comfortable.

On the way back to our room, I noticed a large plastic-upholstered, coin-operated chair in the hall. For 100 yen, it would massage your back and vibrate soothingly. A sign over a small souvenir shop, now closed, announced this temple to be a member of the Japan Tourist Hotel Association.

I slept restlessly, puzzled by what we had gotten ourselves into. Perhaps Koyasan was an important holy place, but it also seemed as worldly and commercial as any motel.

In the middle of the night the kerosene heater ran out of oil, its small red eye faded and the floor grew hard with the cold.

Dawn tinted the room with faint pinks and gold, the sun slanting through red maples outside the window. Parchment walls were washed in pastel light and then, suddenly, they were penetrated with pure rays of sound, the quivering notes of the temple's bells. I had been ready to get up, but now I lay still, listening. Through the thin wood-and-paper skeleton of the monastery I could hear the low, murmuring chants of monks, an unfamiliar babble of prayer accompanied by the pulse of the old bronze bells.

Koyasan had ceased to be a motel.

After a traditional (one table) Japanese breakfast of soup and fish we walked through the small village that is surrounded by the many temples and holy places of the Shingon sect. The morning air was cold and mountain clear, spiced now and then with the sweet perfume of cedar woodsmoke. At eight o'clock, a public address speaker on the main street played some cheerful Japanese music followed by a woman's voice. I asked Hamano what she said.

"She is talking to the children of the town," he explained. "She is telling them to be careful on their way to school, to be good boys and girls and to have a nice day."

Just as the approaches to the Vatican are lined with shops selling blessed religious objects and souvenirs of Rome, so is the small main street of Koyasan. A million Japanese pilgrims a year come here to see the mausoleum of the great St. Kobo deep in a forest of towering cryptomeria trees at the edge of town. Most of the great trees are hundreds of years old, some were supposedly planted by the famous monk himself over a thousand years ago. They form an awesome guard of honor along a mile-long pedestrian path leading to the inner sanctum of Shingon Buddhism.

"St. Kobo was not only the founder of Shingon," Hamano explained, "but sometimes we say that he was also the father of the travel industry in Japan. Everywhere we go in this country, we find places where he planted his trees and did his missionary work ten centuries ago. He was a remarkable traveler."

We walked quietly in the hush of the forest, feeling dwarfed by the giant trees. On either side of the path, gray granite tombs covered with ages of green moss mark the final resting places of rich and famous Japanese over several centuries. If you are a Shingon Buddhist and can afford it, this is the most honored burial place you can have—and the closer to St. Kobo's own mausoleum the better.

"Of course many believe that he is not dead," Hamano said. "He is thought to be in his tomb in deep meditation."

The mausoleum, when we arrived there, was small and rustic, a squarish wooden building with a single door and no windows, looking like a summer cottage closed for the season. Other, more elaborate buildings stand nearby in the filtered light on the forest floor—a temple, a ceremonial hall, a charnel house for the ashes of the faithful. But the ancient trees, nature's majestic pillars, are Kobo's real cathedral.

Beyond the sanctum and out in the sunshine of the 1970s again, we walked past rows of modern memorials constructed in recent years by some of Japan's leading industrial firms to honor deceased workers. A refrigeration company, an automobile manufacturer, a rubber company and a photography firm are some who have erected contemporary monuments in this annex to Kobo's shrine. One is complete with an electric clock. Another is made prominent with a full-scale, brightly painted space rocket. A beggar with a wooden leg sat in front of this one, his pants leg rolled up to show his stump. A pretty young Japanese girl wearing a T-shirt lettered with the words "HONOLULU BOEING 747" dropped a few coins in his hat.

Koyasan seemed to insist on contradictions.

We went back to the monastery to pay our bill. To complete my experience, I still hoped to see a monk in his robes, but there was none in sight. A red Honda motorcycle was parked at the door of the temple. The young man in the *Giants* jacket took our payment and saw that our troublesome baggage was ready for departure.

"Ask him if he is a monk," I said to Hamano on a hunch.

The young man answered my question without translation.

"Yes," said Hamano, a little surprised. "He says he is a monk. He also speaks English."

Atop the holy mountain, as in Japan itself, legends of another time coexist with the realities of today.

CHAPTER 5
Arabian Notebook

I WAS ON my way to Riyadh, capital of Saudi Arabia, a country which does not permit the entry of tourists, but now more than ever admits visitors who come on business. The restricted privilege of just being let in makes Saudi Arabia different, adds an element of adventure to being there. So does the airport sign which says that passengers who refuse to disarm will not be allowed to board Saudi Arabian Airlines planes. I was armed with only cameras and a tape recorder.

In the soft-lighted interior of the DC9, an old Bedouin sat in a window seat across the aisle and looked out at lightning flashes which illuminated the great desert below. In this country, I thought, it could be the first flight of his life or merely his first flight this week. He had a strong, dignified face framed by a red and white checked ghutra which was wrapped softly around his head and neck. The voluminous folds of a brown cape with a gold embroidered collar were drawn around him. His wide, leathery feet in heavy sandals looked somehow out of place on the plush carpeting of a commercial jet. He was a

man of the desert on his way to the big city. He might even be
going to have an audience with his king. It happens in Saudi
Arabia.

Behind the Bedouin, two Japanese businessmen in dark suits
and white shirts finished their meal, brought identical gray
plastic briefcases to their laps and talked excitedly as they
shuffled papers and used their pocket calculators. They were
from a remote culture, too, yet like the rest of us they were on
their way to Riyadh, probably to do business with one of the
king's ministers.

Across the jetliner aisle from the Japanese were two Arab
women, one with a small child sleeping in her lap. They mur-
mured privately to each other beneath black veils which all but
obscured their faces. They were not old women hiding from the
world, but young wives, their fingers carefully manicured and
glittering with gold rings, their dresses modishly short beneath
the all-covering black shrouds that Islam dictates in public. The
baby cried and the mother tossed back her veil to caress the
child. She wore heavy eye shadow and was quite beautiful. By
their appearance I guessed that the two women might be the
wives of rising young officials in Saudi Arabia's expanding
bureaucracy.

Meanwhile this night, in the desert darkness below, the king
himself was reported to be on his way to Riyadh, traveling by
automobile from Jiddah, the old seaport on the Red Sea, via
Taif in the cool mountains, then overland for hundreds of miles
on a road as straight as a pipeline.

"It will take him at least two days," I was told. "He will no
doubt stop one night in the desert, he often does. His tents are
always sent ahead."

I imagined a large encampment with many guards. "Not at
all," my Arab friend said. "A few soldiers, yes, but not many.

He is a modest man, this king. No Cadillacs or Mercedes for him. He travels in an Oldsmobile. It is air-conditioned, of course."

Faisal, King of Arabia, protector of Islam and keeper of its Holy Places, proprietor of a vast subterranean treasure of crude oil, a Bedouin king in a jet age, rich beyond measure, but still faithful to the ways of his ancestors, still comfortable in a tent.

As world capitals go, Riyadh is a small, dusty city with a feeling of frontier about it, of having grown too fast for its many young, newly planted palm trees to catch up. Broad avenues are lined with office buildings and modern government ministries, but some streets end abruptly at the desert's edge as if the city's planners had suddenly decided to expand in another direction.

To Saudis, their capital represents all that is progressive and exciting about their young country. Seventy years ago, Riyadh was just a settlement of mud houses huddled around a Turkish fort in the middle of a flinty plain. Twenty-five years ago, when Faisal's father was king, the "city" was still one of tawny, crenelated buildings and a single big mud palace. Today, with a population of about 300,000, Riyadh has discovered glass walls and cinder block and reinforced concrete and fluorescent lighting and traffic jams and new international hotels. Most fascinating for a visitor is the thought that Riyadh is the seat of such great power, the place where a king and his ministers make the heady plans to spend Saudi Arabia into becoming a modern nation—where oil is turned into gold and gold into everything else that a developing society needs.

It is going to be an interesting process for the rest of the world to watch. Unlike most other emerging nations, Saudi Arabia embarks on her great odyssey with hardly a concern about other societies' most vexing and common problems: shortage of money or surplus of population. Here, on 860,000 square miles of largely uninhabited territory, there is but a thin line of Arabs, 6 million perhaps, no one is really sure. As for the wealth, everybody knows where that comes from.

Saudi Arabia is such a vast, unpainted canvas that the few images one finds on it can be vivid and memorable. Although my reporter's notebooks quickly filled with historical and business facts, socioeconomic trends and geological speculations, my eye roamed beyond my assignment to collect personal pictures of the desert kingdom. Like the passengers on the flight to Riyadh, these are sometimes unrelated and uninterpreted, but they form a haunting montage.

◆ ◆ ◆

I remember the gold souk in Dammam on the Persian Gulf, a narrow labyrinth of streets lined with jewelry shops, each window ablaze with 22-carat gold ornaments under hot spotlights, each small sales counter equipped with a balance scale, each proprietor smiling an invitation in his doorway. Arab women in pairs, dark shapes behind veils, moved from window to window, searching for the same illusion of beauty that women seek in the Place Vendome or on Fifth Avenue.

I remember a long drive to Hofuf to see the camel market and to hear the bidding of desert Arabs for these strange animals —which Saudis will assure you are fast being replaced by Japanese pickup trucks. Hofuf could be the Old West without board sidewalks, a place where caravan routes have crossed for centuries, a trader's town with unpaved streets that swarm with donkey carts and people. We found the camel market closed, the animals penned into a walled enclosure, the auctioneer complaining that there were no buyers today. For a few riyals he opened the gate and let us take pictures, holding the animals' heads this way and that to oblige, but looking sad all the while because he knew we weren't going to buy a camel.

I remember water in the midst of the dry desert, giant subterranean rivers boiling up out of the ground at a green oasis called Al Hasa, the biggest in the country. One of these springs, the Ain Khudud, delivers 27,000 gallons per minute, a sweet torrent that has flowed undiminished for centuries. Saudis wash their clothes and their bodies at the springs. Young boys dive into the big pools to get wet, then climb out and dump Tide detergent on each other from head to foot before lathering.

Swiss engineers and German contractors have built a 1000-mile irrigation system in Al Hasa for the Saudi government, an elaborate maze of pre-cast, V-shaped concrete aquaducts which carry life-giving water to 50,000 acres of dates, onions, eggplant, tomatoes, alfalfa, cucumbers, cabbage and anything else the ambitious agronomists want to try. Just beyond the last drink of water, the sands of the desert drift around the oasis, circling what was once theirs as if they would like to take it back.

I remember "nightclubs" in the desert—a shack by the road, a few weathered tables and chairs out in the sand and sometimes a fence all around for privacy. A place for a man to go after a hot day to enjoy a Pepsi-Cola, a cool after-sunset breeze and maybe watch a little outdoor television. In some parts of the world, it might be called a taverna, in others a pub. By any name, it is a place for companionship and sociability. A man doesn't have to be an Arab to be welcome. Just don't bring your wife—or ask for a beer.

I remember a well-polished Mercedes parked by the side of the road many miles from anywhere. A few yards away, kneeling alone in the sands, was its driver. It was time for evening prayer. The man bowed low many times while his car's emergency flashers blinked impatiently.

I remember the red sand dunes of the Dahna desert, looking

like a turbulent ocean from the air and like the landscape of the moon when the DC3 put us down in the middle of nowhere. Men are still looking for new oil under all this sand, living on their own life-support systems in trailer camps—drill bosses and engineers and geologists and mud specialists and rough-necks alike, a close-mouthed bunch of Okies and Texans, all reading the same dog-eared paperbacks, shooting a little pool and saying nothing to strangers.

I remember stopping with my friend Muhammad to share a box lunch by the side of the road. We parked our white Pontiac well off the two-lane blacktop that extended from horizon to horizon with no other man-made object in sight. The road was survey-straight, but rising and falling gently like a long, narrow carpet laid over the undulations of the sands. There was no traffic except an occasional heavy truck which would first be-come visible as a black spot suspended in mid-air over the highway's distant vanishing point, an upside down exclamation mark, a mirage which shimmered for many minutes before the vehicle itself materialized.

"Vegetables from Lebanon," Muhammad said as the big diesel thundered by, its body panels decorated with primitive, colorful murals painted by the driver, a plume of smoke coming from its exhaust stack.

We walked some distance away from the car and into the sands, two people on a big beach, looking for a good place to spread the blanket. Finally, we sat in the lee of a small dune where a few flowers had emerged, the result of a recent rain. Muhammad named them as easily as I could have identified a lilac for him in Massachusetts.

We ate the company lunch without much conversation. Sandwiches, hard boiled egg, Sunkist orange, warm soda from a can.

Later, Muhammad napped briefly in the sun and I looked around for the car and couldn't see it in any direction. Which way had we come? Which way had I turned? For a moment, fantasy took over: I was alone in the middle of the world's biggest desert. Then I stood up and, of course, there was the Pontiac, just over the dunes, looking like a piece of space hardware abandoned by an earlier expedition.

I remember a conversation about the great desert caravans of the past and I asked a young Saudi friend how fast a camel walks. He looked at me as if I had asked for the answer to a complex formula in chemistry, but he said he would try to find out. He asked several other people in his office and they said the question must be a joke. Finally, someone came up with an answer.

"They say a camel walks 4 miles an hour," my friend reported, "but we hope you realize that such a fact is irrelevant in Saudi Arabia today."

CHAPTER 6

Macau—They Say It's Portuguese

THE AGED Nissan taxi struggled uphill in the rain, lurching from ruts to holes like a broken beetle making its way toward death. Reddish mud ran in small rivers down each side of the road while a curtain of water slashed against the windshield. The wipers were not working.

"We shall soon have a new road up here," my Chinese friend said. "The Portuguese have always been great builders. Some of the cobblestone roads here in Macau were laid 400 years ago. The stones were brought from Portugal as ballast in sailing ships."

Macau clings to Portugal and Portugal clings to Macau. Half a world apart, the motherland and its tiny overseas province on the south China coast dance a courtly minuet and pretend that the world hasn't really changed too much since Jorge Alvarez discovered the place in 1513. There may be troubles in Angola, but there is tranquility in Macau. Cobblestones and Fado. Pousadas. Mateus wine. Houses painted in Mediterranean pastels facing the China Sea. The tourist folders call it the Latin

47

Orient. Quiet. Going nowhere. In no hurry to get there.

A long time ago, someone smashed the nose and broke the arm of Jorge Alvarez' stone statue in the main square. It has not been repaired.

"Of course, things are much different here on the islands," my friend observed. "Macau is crowded and fast-paced, but this is the country." The Nissan diesel labored upward, gasping in low gear now, moving slow enough for the driver to reach out and say hello to his friends passing along the steep road. Some of them seemed pleased to see that he had rich clients this morning.

The islands are Taipa and Coloane, small, green and hilly, one and two miles square, reached by ferry from Macau. Macau itself, an island attached to the Chinese mainland by a causeway, is a city of 300,000 persons, 99 percent Chinese. Only 5000 live on the islands. They inhabit a few villages where there are some telephones, some electricity and a water shortage. For transport there are two ancient Bedford busses with the front fenders removed. And the Nissan taxi. The back seat was tightly upholstered in clear plastic slip covers. There were lace antimacassars underneath the plastic, neat and white.

Macau is a place where people from busy British Hong Kong come to get away from it all. The islands are where people go to get away from the "fast pace" of Portuguese Macau.

"The government has a plan to relieve the population pressure in Macau by developing Taipa and Coloane—one for industry and one for tourism." The driver pointed to a motel-like structure built into the hillside ahead. "Our newest tourist hotel —the Pousada Coloane."

I had heard about the plan for the islands from a man who lives in Macau. "Once a year," he explained, "representatives of the colony go back to Lisbon to tell the government about their great plans for the growth of Macau. The government listens and approves and the representatives come back here secure in their jobs and ready for another year of doing nothing. They've been talking about building a bridge from here to the islands for seven years. Now the Chinese are doing it for them." Siesta in Macau. Part of its appeal.

About 1½ million visitors a year come to this Latin Orient, most of them wealthy Chinese from Hong Kong, 40 miles away. But there were also 300,000 foreign devils. The Chinese come to gamble; the tourists come for the day, persuaded by their travel agents that the place is a must—one of the "seven stars of the east," an unforgettable experience. Macau is a side trip from Hong Kong where five companies offer tours: for a package price you get a round trip on a 40 mph hydrofoil boat, sightseeing, lunch, a shopping tour—and 45 minutes in a casino. It's not enough time to see much, eat much or gamble much, but then, the casino managements aren't really interested in tourist dollars. Fat cat Chinese are the big customers. They come by the thousands on weekends.

The rain let up briefly as we reached the Pousada Coloane. Silver-gray shreds of cloud slipped down the mountainsides. From the terrace, where bright colored umbrellas were furled dismally in the wet, we could look across Cheoc Van Bay to the barren hills of Communist China. The manager apologized. Lunch might be delayed. There had been a power failure. "We don't have enough electricity here," he explained. A few lights in the dining room burned dimly like embers. A small lizard scurried up the wall. The Nissan driver went into the kitchen for some food. We sat on a broad porch sheltered from the rain. There were no other guests.

The Pousada is charming—and cheap. The decor is distinctly Portuguese. There are only 12 rooms, all air-conditioned. With this you get a great beach and a great view and the feeling of being in a place where the Internal Revenue Service would never find you in a thousand years.

"The syndicate protects you here," my host said. You waited for him to smile at his own jest, but he didn't. The syndicate is no jest. It runs the Pousada Coloane. And the Pousada Macau. It runs the casinos—the Estoril and the Palace and all the others. It runs the big hotels. It runs the hydrofoils that bring you here and the ferries that will take you back. In short, it runs Macau like a surrogate government. It is spoken of openly—not like the capital-S Syndicate in the U.S. In Macau it is a benefactor: the Macau Tourism and Amusements Company, chartered for 23 years by the Portuguese government in 1961.

"Whenever the community needs a donation," my friend explained, "they can come to the syndicate and never be refused." The syndicate is four men—two Chinese, one Indo-Chinese, one Portuguese-Chinese. They head four families. Each family has domain over some aspect of the syndicate's operations. Without the syndicate, Macau would assuredly be poorer than it is. But it is good works rather than gambling that the syndicate wishes to be remembered for: a convent here, an orphanage there. Money for schools, money for the poor, money for medicine. Money which arrives every weekend by hydrofoil from Hong Kong in the pockets of rich Chinese—pounds, dollars, even gold. The yellow stuff is traded openly in Macau; you can buy it, sell it, melt it down, or turn it into 24-carat jewelry, all perfectly legal as far as Portugal or the syndicate is concerned.

The cold bottle of white Portuguese wine stood in a pool of its own condensation on the table. The air was heavy and sweet with the smell of blossoms. A distant, stroboscopic blink of lightning reminded me of the lyric about dawn coming up like thunder out of China 'cross the bay.

"That's where your steamed prawns came from—over there across the bay," my host said. "Right off a Communist junk a few hours ago, no doubt." They were delicious in hot pepper sauce with green salad. Most of Macau's food comes from the Chinese mainland. A Chinese navy landing craft ferries much of it across to Taipa every morning.

After lunch we came down the mountain and into the town of Coloane, a collection of small houses, sleeping dogs, work-shops, automobiles without wheels, stores; its streets scrambling with children, chickens, bicycles, goats, young men in undershirts and pajama bottoms running with baskets balanced on the ends of shoulder poles and old Chinese ladies in black pajama suits walking slowly under black umbrellas. Although there are no Portuguese on Coloane, the soft drink advertisements say "Beba Fanta Grape" and "Beba Coca-Cola."

"Do the Chinese ever learn any Portuguese?" I asked.

"Never. But old Portuguese families sometimes take a Chinese name."

The red and green flag of Portugal flies over Macau, but 300,000 Chinese (a) can't be wrong and (b) don't give a damn.

A mile-long concrete bridge connects Coloane with Taipa. It is low, flat and straight, built on pilings driven into shallow water. The taxi driver crossed at 15 mph. I asked if there was a speed limit. "No," said my host, "he just wants you to see the bridge." It had taken several years to build, I was told. Then, shortly after it was opened with considerable ceremony, portions of the roadway collapsed and it had to be rebuilt. This melodramatic history notwithstanding, a motorist could see all he needed of the bridge even at 60 mph.

Taipa is like Coloane except for the firecracker factories.

Special permission was required to enter one. No smoke and no camera flash, I was told. We passed through a gate in a high wall and into an enclosure where there were many small stone and plaster buildings. Between each building and the next was a tapering concrete wall, eight feet high, two feet thick at the base, thinner at the top. In each of the buildings whole families of people, men, women and small children, completed steps in the process of making the firecrackers. There were no lights. Metal shutters on the windows were open. One man worked with a lighted cigarette dangling from his lips. No smoke. No flash.

"Last year, six of these people were killed by an explosion," my friend told me. "It would have been worse without the walls between the buildings to stop the blast. They found one man's head fifty yards away.

"Someone is killed every year, but these families would not do anything else. They earn good money because of the danger —about $1.70 per day."

They also have a pool to swim in. For emergency use only. It is muddy and shallow, but in case of fire everyone jumps in, takes a deep breath and holds his head under water until after the explosion.

Another flicker of lightning and roll of thunder. "They will probably go home now. They never work when there is a storm."

In the courtyard, surrounded by the buildings, was a quarter acre of finished firecrackers laid on racks to cure in the sun. They were covered with tarpaulins now because of the rain. "But the canvas doesn't stop lightning," I pointed out. My friend shrugged. People have to have firecrackers.

The Nissan took us to the ferry and the ferry took us back to Macau. We passed the small, gray Chinese gunboat that patrols the western edge of Macau's harbor. There was laundry flying on the foredeck and a red flag at the stern.

Much has been said about Macau living under the gun of Communist China. Dramatic stories are written about a truculent Mao Tse Tung threatening to swallow imperialist-dog Portugal's colony with a single, fiery dragon's-gulp. An old bromide says that Mao could take Macau with a phone call. Undoubtedly. But there is, nevertheless, no doomsday quality to life there. In confrontations with the Chinese during the 1960s, the Portuguese always backed down. Nowadays, according to one westerner in Macau, "The Portuguese don't even issue a weather forecast without clearing it with China."

Macau may, as some say, be useful to China as a free port and window on the world. For whatever reason, the community does live without fear. The Portuguese governor is usually an army officer. Every Sunday morning, at a secret meeting in a secret, underground war room, he presides over a full dress meeting of army officers to plan the defense of Macau in case the Chinese attack. Some say the plans consist largely of how best to get the syndicate's money out of the casinos and onto three Portuguese Navy gunboats for prompt shipment to a Swiss bank.

From the ferry we took a pedicab back to the hotel—a tricycle with the driver up front and a rickshaw-style seat for two at the rear. A ride, short or long, is two Macau dollars—36¢ —and solicitation by cruising pedicab drivers is lively. At the end of the trip they will ask three dollars and say thank you when you give them two.

The doorman at the Hotel Lisboa is dressed in a bright brocaded vest, black knee britches, white stockings and buckles on his shoes. He opens the glass portals on what the syndicate believes is the most elegant and opulent hotel in the Orient. The lobby is a full-circle amphitheatre large enough for the Clyde Beatty circus, complete with elephants and aerial acts. A domed mosaic ceiling depicts the voyages of the Portuguese navigators of the 15th Century. The giant crystal chandelier ("imported from Germany at the great cost of $48,000," you are told) hangs over a huge circular carpet—65 feet in diameter, woven in Red China from good Australian wool and spread on a rubber base so spongey that a walk across the lobby feels like a stroll on a trampoline. There is no furniture—only cavernous grandeur with the sky above and the rug below.

One bitterly objective observer says, "The Lisboa was designed by an architect who had never seen Las Vegas but thought he knew what it should look like."

Like it or not, the Lisboa is the syndicate's—and hence Macau's—showplace. It rises at the water's edge, a circular tower the color of ripe papaya, crowned at its summit with a burst of gilded balls resembling a model of atomic particles, its exterior floodlighted at night like an amusement park rollercoaster. It dominates the Macau skyline as much as its 300 rooms and its casinos and restaurants dominate the tourist scene.

There are other hotels in Macau, to be sure—the Estoril, the Matsuya, the Caravella (all syndicate owned)—but the big, new Lisboa is *it;* full to overflowing every weekend, echoingly empty during the week. A single room costs very little but suites can be expensive. The management now allows only one extra cot to be moved into any room. It seems some Chinese weekenders from Hong Kong were renting suites and then asking for eight extra cots, please.

Water, according to the Lisboa directory, is available, hot or cold, on a 24-hour basis in your bathroom, although power failures sometimes cut off the supply above the seventh floor. Air conditioning is also promised, electricity permitting, on a

24-hour basis. The rooms are as cold as meat lockers, but temperatures are uncertain in other parts of the hotel. So great are the variations sometimes that eyeglasses and camera lenses fog over with condensed humidity.

Automatic elevators stop and go with a will of their own. Bellboys are instructed always to ride with guests in case of equipment failure.

For all its comic-opera failings, it must be conceded that the Lisboa is not so much a hotel for world tourists as it is a casino for gamblers with rooms upstairs. Modern Japanese escalators deliver the customers from the lobby to a lower level where the casino, unlike the water and the air conditioning, operates 24 hours a day. Like the lobby, it is a vast circular cavern, heavily carpeted, intimately lighted and furnished with tables for roulette, fan tan, craps, Black Jack and the most popular game with the Chinese, Big & Small. On weekends the room throbs with action; during the week most of the tables are deserted except for some shirtsleeve Chinese.

"The really high rollers play during the week," you are told. Bets are limited to 2000 Macau dollars—about $400—and go down to 10¢ in the one-arm bandits.

What percentage does the house take? One man in the hotel says the syndicate can't be taking too big a cut or the gamblers would stop coming. But the management concedes that 90 percent of its guests lose. "You see," said the hotel public relations man, "you can never have enough money to win. The bank is always bigger than you are."

The Lisboa is not the only place where you can lose. Go out into the sweet night and take a walk along the Avenida Ribeiro until you come to the inner harbor. There, in all its gaudy glory, is the Macau Palace, a floating casino, three stories high, moored permanently to the dockside. Inside there is a restaurant with continuous performances of Chinese opera and a bar with a rock group. "Buckaroo" one-arm bandits are labeled "guaranteed jackpot," but there is also a discreet sign on the wall which says, "NO ONE CAN WIN ALL THE TIME. WE ADVISE YOU TO PLAY MERELY FOR PLEASURE AND RISK ONLY WHAT YOU CAN SPARE. *The Management.*"

Because the syndicate's various casinos never close their doors, they employ almost 4000 people in shifts—a not inconsiderable factor in Macau's economy. "The syndicate puts more money into this place than Portugal does," one man tells you, but there is still not enough money to provide free schools for Macau's children. Private school fees average about $5 a month —an impossible figure for most Chinese.

Nothing keeps the Chinese from leaving Macau if they wish, of course, but like their brothers in colonial Hong Kong, many seem to have a pragmatic indifference to what flag flies over their head. At the Porto do Cerco—the barrier gate between sovereign Portugal and the People's Republic of China where both flags fly—Macau Chinese move freely back and forth across the border while western visitors may not approach within 100 yards. It was late afternoon when I went there. A Portuguese policeman in khaki shorts barred the way. Nearby, souvenir stands make a living from foreign tourists who take some small but delicious thrill from looking down the road at The Enemy. Copies of Chairman Mao's little red book were on sale for 36¢. I bought one in English language with a washable plastic cover. The shopkeeper asked me if I wanted to buy any nude postage stamps. These turned out to be pictures of ladies like Minerva with one breast bared. There were also "Chinese antiquities" available, some undoubtedly from across the border, some counterfeited last night in Macau. Film. Postcards. Pictures of Mao. Beba Coca-Cola.

A few Chinese were moving toward me along the road from China. They carried their personal possessions in plastic shopping bags. On their shirts they wore the red badge of Mao.

"Who are they?" I asked my guide.

"Just Chinese who have been on vacation. Probably visiting relatives in China."

"What are the chances that they are Communist?"

My friend shrugged. "Watch them take their Mao badges off their shirts when they cross the border and then tell me what their politics are. Over the centuries, we Chinese have learned survival. To survive here you wear a badge on one side of the line, you take it off on the other."

We left the border and drove a short distance down a dirt road. "Would you like to see one of the Red guards up close? I know a place where tourists are never taken—just here where the bamboo fence is across the road. Keep your camera out of sight."

There was a yellow sentry box only a few feet away. Smoke from a nearby trash fire filled the air. Two Chinese soldiers with guns stopped to look at our car. We backed up slowly and drove away. I felt nothing—except perhaps sympathy for the men who had to muck around with rifles on their shoulders next to a garbage dump, guarding against . . . what?

If Macau's back is to the Chinese colossus, her face is to the sea and her most beautiful feature is her elegant old seafront road, the Praia Grande. This curving, tree-lined avenue faced with pink, green and blue stucco houses is the one part of the colony which best lives up to the Latin Orient image. Century-old banyan trees, their trunks enfolded like the skin on an old man's neck, lean over the seawall and are reflected in the water. In May, the flame trees, ablaze with red blossoms, mix their color with the greens of bamboo and banyan. Red and white geraniums tumble from windowboxes and pots.

Midway along the Praia Grande is the quaint old Pousada Macau, known for good food, including a spicy African chicken dish transplanted from Portugal's African colonies. Macau sole, as famous as Dover sole and just as good, is another specialty. The wines are cheap and enjoyable and a luncheon on the crisp white enclosed porch is one of the most pleasant meals you can find in Macau.

A little further along the Praia Grande there is a large rock close inshore which seems to sit crouched in the water like a giant frog about to leap. Indeed, so real did this threat seem to a wealthy Chinese whose house faced the frog that he feared the creature would come ashore some moonless night and devour his fortune.

In situations like this, Chinese do not consult civil authorities, they turn to a geomancy man for advice.

"I see," said the geomancy man, "that the frog has a large mouth."

"Yes," said the wealthy man, "he will eat my money with it."

"Then the mouth should be cemented shut," advised the geomancy man—and so it was done and the giant frog sits there to this day, his wide smiling mouth stuffed with cement.

Nearby, a Portuguese soldier stands guard with fixed bayonet at the governor's palace. The Chinese regard him as powerless against the frog compared to the word of the geomancy man.

I had come from Hong Kong on the hydrofoil—a swift, bumpy ride of an hour and a quarter. "But you should go home on the *S.S. Macau,*" I was told. "She is slower, but as soon as she gets out of Portuguese territorial waters, they present the best strip show in the Orient . . ."

The *Macau* is called a ferry, but she is more like a small ocean steamer. I booked a stateroom, bought tickets for the

"Parisian Burlesque" and went aboard. As we sailed, the few dim lights of Macau slipped astern and faded quickly. Only the Lisboa stood out like a beacon. I remembered Esmeralda who sang sad Fado numbers in a dark room where there were only four paying customers; I remembered the bored young girls behind the tables in the casinos, all in uniform lavender cheongsams supplied by the syndicate; I remembered the song of a junk man on Taipa, moving from house to house offering to buy "old watches and broken jade."

♦   ♦   ♦

"Well, how did you like Macau?" they asked me when I was back in Hong Kong the next day.

"It's not all that bad after you get used to it," I was told. "Of course, the Lisboa is absurd, but we don't ever stay there. If you want to get away from it all, the pousadas are nice . . ."

CHAPTER 7
Czechoslovakia

IN THE POLITICAL nomenclature of our time, Czechoslovakia is an "East bloc nation," a "Socialist republic," a
"Warsaw Pact member," a Russian "satellite," an "Iron Curtain country." If you ask your travel agent if all this makes the
CSSR an alien and risky land for travel, he will no doubt assure
you that it does not. Czechoslovakia is not really "east," after
all, but the heartland of Europe, a country of great scenic
variety where 3000 castles and chateaux and 40,000 other
buildings have been designated as historic treasures, where music and the arts thrive, where sports are well-organized and
folklore is rich. What more could a traveler ask?

He could ask about something else that every country creates
—an atmosphere, a feeling. Happy, carefree Italy. Proper,
punctual Switzerland. What is the feeling in Czechoslovakia? Is
it a place where the mood is relaxed or fearful? Don't politics
make a difference?

"When political tensions flare up," says a spokesman for
the Czech tourist office in Prague, "we suffer cancellations.

We realize that there are always a few tourists who are afraid."

◆   ◆   ◆

For the U.S. couple, the most fearful thing had happened: their passports were gone. Panicky pawing through briefcase and pockets confirmed it. The last hotel still held the little blue-green books—but the Americans were now halfway across the country in their travels. Worse, they knew, this wasn't friendly old London or sunny Roma. It was communist Czechoslovakia. To anxious Americans, thousands of miles from their reassuring travel agents, Czech police can look very much like Russian soldiers.

◆   ◆   ◆

One Russian soldier sleeps forever on a hill above Bratislava. A visitor's eye just happens to fall on his name out of all the others. It is cut in Cyrillic letters on black granite: Ivan Ivanovich Sulga. He died the first week in May 1945, probably in his twenties. He rests with 6346 of his Russian comrades at a majestic memorial called Slavin. Tourists go there on sunny days for a fine view of Slovakia's capital city and the Danube flowing below. Young Czech lovers come, too, walking hand in hand among the graves of the known and the unknown. Some leave flowers on an altar of marble beneath a blood-red star formed from rough chunks of famed Czech crystal. There is no politics here. The men who died fighting the Nazi tyranny are simply dead.

The last that Lieutenant Sulga saw of Bratislava on his final day in May was a city of rubble, fiercely defended by retreating Germans. Today, Bratislava is rebuilt, the third largest city in Czechoslovakia. Seen from the mass grave of Slavin, one of the most prominent landmarks of the new city is an 18-story tourist hotel called the Kiev. It is usually full of Germans.

◆   ◆   ◆

Tourism is booming in Czechoslovakia, but if there is a catch in this claim, it may be that most of these travelers come from other Iron Curtain countries. They visit Czechoslovakia because they are not allowed to travel outside the boundaries of their East Bloc. The others come from the outside to look in. Most are from western Europe, a few from the U.S; almost all of them in groups which "do" the country in three days and move on. They see Hradcany castle, a chateau or two in the country and spend half a day shopping near Prague's Golden Cross for porcelains and crystal. They miss a lot. Czechoslovakia is worth a longer look.

◆ ◆ ◆

The policeman looked bleakly at the American couple while their guide, a representative of Cedok, the Czech national tourist agency, made explanations in their behalf. The passports, he said, had been left behind at the last hotel. But without them, it was not possible to register at any other hotel. Could a special permission be given? Some temporary papers?

A photo of Czech president Ludwig Svoboda looked down from the wall. The police officer, with three silver stars on red shoulder boards, studied his countryman as suspiciously as he did the Americans. The man from Cedok sensed this and handed over his own identity papers. The photo in the little red book was taken when he was 15—which is when every Czech must begin carrying his proof of existence.

◆ ◆ ◆

Cedok is everywhere in Czechoslovakia. As a government agency, it owns all the hotels in the country, old and new, and books almost all the tours, whether for groups or individuals. It has offices in every city and a representative connected with almost every hotel. It also acts as a travel agency for Czechs traveling abroad. Out of 14½ million Czechs, only a bus load or two ever come to the U.S. on a Cedok tour.

"It is very expensive to go to the U.S.," a Cedok spokesman explains.

It is not very expensive to travel in the CSSR. Prices are government regulated in this "new and just social order." There is one scale of hotel prices for tourists and a lower scale of prices for Czech citizens. Cedok does not book Americans in less than "first class" accommodations, having correctly concluded that what is called first class in spartan Czechslovakia is only average in the United States.

Food is also a regulated bargain. Cuisine may not be one of the country's strong points, but the meals are hearty and heavy and the meat content of restaurant dishes is usually specified (in grams) on the menu, so you always know what you're going to get for your money. The ever-present 100-gram (3½ oz.) beef goulash may take many and surprising forms in the CSSR, but if the menu says it contains 100 grams of meat, comrade, then it's 100 grams you get. Honest weight—no springs.

Your travel agent may tell you that a no-tipping rule in Czechoslovakia will help hold down your costs. Don't believe him. Although socialist dogma teaches that tipping is demeaning to both the giver and the receiver, tips are nevertheless expected throughout the CSSR. Service, however, has an indifferent quality almost everywhere. Most waiters display all the graces of underpaid civil servants. In spite of all this, failure to put some coins into the upturned palms of porters, hair dressers, check room attendants, lavatory personnel and doormen will usually produce the same cold stares and dark mutterings that one would get in New York or Paris.

◆　◆　◆

Old Prague, the historic center, is a beautiful city, ornamented by great varieties in architecture, landscaped by the broad and graceful River Vltava. It is a place of many bridges and church towers and castles on hilltops. Its museums and libraries and concert halls reflect centuries of culture. Its streets and squares and public parks are broom-clean and litter free. Brilliant posters announce entertainments and sports events. Flags fly everywhere, from public buildings, lamp posts, even on busses and trolley cars—the red, white and blue tri-color of the Czech nation, often side by side with the hammer and sickle flag of the Soviet union and the plain red banners of communism. When they snap in a fresh breeze, they seem to be celebrating something.

But the streets of Prague are dark at night, as if mourning the accumulated tragedies of Czech history. From the Hapsburgs to Hitler to the present, this ancient capital has endured the rule of others and when evening comes, gaiety dims. Trolley cars growl slowly through the cobbled squares, their yellow eyes reflecting weakly on polished rails, their bells curiously silent. Occasional electric arcs from the overhead wires illuminate the baroque façades of old buildings with momentary light, like a war-time flare. Even in famed Wenceslas Square, center of Prague's tourist area, there is a feeling of enforced brownout, of a winter's night come too soon. It is not a square, anyway, but a broad avenue with Champs Elysees pretentions. The trolley cars run up and down the middle and on both sides there are hotels, airline offices, candy shops, book stores, a motorcycle agency, a store selling records and tapes (no rock music allowed) and a small department store.

The show windows of Dum Mody appeared in the background of many news photos when Soviet tanks rolled into Prague on August 21, 1968, to put an end to what Alexander Dubcek had called "communism with a human face." The tanks parked in front of Dum Mody and at the foot of the statue of Good King Wenceslas and young Czechs screamed hatred at the impassive Russian soldiers who manned them. The store was closed for several days. When it opened again, Dubcek was gone, but the Russians stayed. There are still 40,000 of them garrisoned in the CSSR according to some estimates, but a traveler will seldom see them, nor will a Czech talk about them.

◆ ◆ ◆

At Lidice, outside Prague, they will show you a film of the first time Soviet tanks came to Czechoslovakia in 1945. (One of them, Number 23, has been permanently preserved as a memorial in Prague.) Lidice was a small farming village of about 500 inhabitants which, at Hitler's order, was wiped from the face of the earth on October 6, 1942. It was a reprisal for the assassination of a German named Heydrich who was the Nazi ruler of the districts of Bohemia and Moravia.

If you are old enough to remember World War II, you may remember Lidice—a mass atrocity that became a rallying cry around the world, a My Lai of its day. One hundred and forty three men, the town's entire male population, were herded into the basement of a school and machine gunned to death, they knew not why. Today, photographs of the victims make a melancholy montage in a small museum and only the breeze whispers across the grassland that was once a town.

The film that tells Lidice's story is shown free and is available in several languages, including English. There are no Americans in the film, only Germans who are shown laughing as the town is dynamited—and then the liberating Russians arriving in their tanks.

Tour groups come to Lidice, even Germans. They see the film and put flowers on the foundation stones of the schoolhouse and take snapshots of the now empty valley.

◆ ◆ ◆

Your Cedok guide will probably tell you on the first day that there is nothing in Czechoslovakia which can not be photographed except "military objects"—which includes men in uniform. National security.

But in the Moser Glass Company showrooms on the road outside Karlovy Vary, photographs are not allowed either.

"We permitted it once," says a company spokesman, "but then the Japanese came here and took pictures and produced copies of our designs within three weeks. Now photos are not allowed." Commercial security.

A visitor may, of course, buy any piece of glass he fancies from Moser and take it out in the parking lot and photograph it. Or take it home to Tokyo. In Czechoslovakia, as elsewhere, money buys, but the camera steals.

Oh, yes. One more thing which must not be photographed. Policemen.

◆   ◆   ◆

The police captain asked what identification the Americans had. Drivers licences and credit cards were put on the counter. Another policeman got up off a cot in the corner to look. It was hard to see the small print in the gloom of the room. The officer with the silver stars took his glasses from his shirt pocket and rubbed the lenses across his stomach.

"What is this date?" he asked. Date of birth, said the man from Connecticut.

The policeman smiled then for the first time and said something in Czech to the man from Cedok.

"He says you are exactly the same age he is," the guide interpreted, and then the policeman and the American looked at each other with a mutual understanding and the officer grinned broadly and everyone in the room knew then that things would probably turn out all right.

◆ ◆ ◆

Czechs say they like Americans. They have relatives in America, they explain, thousands of kinfolk around Chee-ka-go. Czechs also like American things. Didn't the Czech writer Franz Kafka do a book called *Amerika?* And didn't Dvorak compose the *Symphony from The New World?* When Pan Am's twice-weekly 707 arrives at Prague's airport, there is a rush of young Czechs to the observation deck to get a good look at a Boeing and the people it brings from abroad. The Russian Tupolevs on the airfield are just as sleek as the U.S. plane, but Pan Am is America. So are western movies, Polaroid cameras, blue jeans, Champion spark plugs, Coca-Cola, pop records, STP, hamburgers with french fries—all dearly coveted in the CSSR. Only a trickle of non-socialist consumer goods gets into Czechoslovakia across what might by now be called the ironic curtain. These few treats from the west are sold only in a chain of government-operated stores called Tuzex. These exist, in part, for the convenience of souvenir-hunting tourists. Also, if you run out of Kodak film or Gillette blades while traveling in the CSSR, you can find them only in a Tuzex. Any Czech who happens to like the shave he gets from a Trac II can buy one, too, of course—but there is a catch. He must pay for it in dollars. For most Czechs, dollars are impossible to acquire. But there are ways.

◆ ◆ ◆

They say the last time a bank was robbed in Czechoslovakia was six years ago and the crooks were caught 20 minutes later. The CSSR is not a place to monkey around with law and order. This has little to do with the police state, however. The people of this land are hardworking, phlegmatic in adversity, peasant-honest and still devout. The rip-off is not one of their ways of life.

"We have no drug problem here," your guide will tell you, "and no street crime. Everyone is safe; there is no cause for fear."

And that may be true, but the voice behind you on the street can sound as frightening as a mugger. "Crowns for dollars?" it propositions as you turn the corner from the Ambassador hotel. You've been spotted for what you are: an American with money —the kind of money Tuzex takes, the kind that can buy genuine Levi Straus jeans, none of that ill-fitting Polish stuff.

The official tourist rate of exchange is 12 crowns to the dollar. On the street, especially at night, you may be offered 20. But be careful. The man offering the deal may be police.

In the 15th Century, true wealth in this part of Europe was measured in a unit called the *tolar*. *Tolar* is the origin of our word dollar—and although 500 years have passed, a dollar still represents true wealth in the CSSR. It is a piece of America; it can buy something American.

American-style long hair and short skirts are deplored by party theoreticians as symbols of western decay which are unbecoming to Czech youth, but there are as many young men with Prince Valiant hair around Prague's Lucerna dance hall as in any U.S. action spot—and Czech girls continue to display some of the best legs in Europe under dancing micro-minis. Yet, if hard rock and pop culture is packing some of Prague's youth into the discotheques, Dvorak is also still alive and well in the hearts of Czechs of all ages.

◆ ◆ ◆

The poster outside the concert hall announced that the Karlovarsky Symfonicky orchestra would perform Dvorak's Opus 104 for violincello this night, followed by a Brahm's requiem. For most small towns in the U.S. it would be a heady program, but this Czech town of 45,000 was Karlovy Vary and, even under socialism, it has class. Karlovy Vary was called Carlsbad before two wars and the new order changed everything. Today, despite all the red stars on the buildings, it is still one of Czechoslovakia's most civilized tourist attractions, a place with an enduring touch of elegance and of history.

For three and a half centuries, the great and near-great of Europe came to this place to "take the waters," to be "cured" by sipping from the hot, mineral-laden springs which flow from over 80 thermal wells in the earth. In the 1600s, nobility arrived in horse drawn carriages and were welcomed to the spa's many hotels by fanfares of trumpets. They brought their own physicians and entire retinues of servants with them and rented large houses or entire floors in hotels and spent "the season." The Emperor Franz Joseph came here and the Shah of Iran and Beethoven and Edward the VII, who dedicated the golf course in 1905.

Today, hundreds of thousands of visitors a year come to Karlovy Vary and although it's a new, proletarian crowd and there are no fanfares, many of the tourists can afford to stay at the old Grand Hotel Moskva-Pupp, perhaps the most gracious hostelry that Cedok was lucky enough to inherit from the past.

Seven hundred persons came to hear Dvorak in the hotel concert hall, an ornate and well-proportioned room with a stage at one end and a balcony all around. The orchestra was pressed and starched in formal black and white and the audience sat under crystal chandeliers, some dressed in evening clothes, some only in sweaters, but all piously attentive to the spell of their beloved music. There were no empty seats. One could not help thinking that if a new holocaust came to Czechoslovakia and swept everything away, as at Lidice, there would be Czechs in this room who would find a way to make violins soon again.

"Are concerts like this popular everywhere?" you ask, and

a Czech friend says music is a part of life in every Czech city, not just fashionable old Carlsbad, but even in some of the "new towns" like industrial Sokolov where electric power is made from strip mined coal and the air is heavy with pollution and the neighborhoods are as gray and grim as a prison.

"They have their own symphony in Sokolov," you are told. "It costs only 40 cents to go."

In the warm sunshine of autumn, Karlovy Vary is a promenade of people from all over the nation and some from the outside world: young and old, healthy and infirm. They stroll under the well-pruned trees along the River Tepla, eating ice cream cones and thin cookies, big as dinner plates, called *oplatky*. In the parking lot of the Grand Hotel, foreign automobiles that are seldom seen in plainer parts of the country attract little groups of lookers, fathers and sons, leaning low to peer into the richly decadent interior of a Mach 1 Ford or considering the Stalinist styling of a big Russian Chaika with Hungarian plates.

Under a long, 19th Century collonade, several of the mineral water springs are piped into ornamental fountains for all to use free of charge and people come to fill small drinking flasks, then continue their strolling, sipping as they go. The water is hot and foul tasting; it is supposed to be good for everything from liver ailments to eczema.

Older generations sit on public benches facing the late sun, eyes closed, hands folded on their laps, as if simply being in this place, so long reserved for the rich and famous, will somehow relieve the aches and pains of their years. In a small park nearby, a heroic statue of Lenin looks down on the scene, appropriating it, as it were, for all the people.

◆   ◆   ◆

There are other spas in the western regions of Czechslovakia —Marianske Lazne (Marienbad) and Frantiskovy Lazne

(Franzenbad) and strange Soos park where the last gasps of a dying volcano push bubbling mud up through gleaming white salt beds. All were fashionable once and all attract tourists today. Whether the waters of these places are truly efficacious is a point which most people don't argue too seriously. There are spas all over Europe, 58 in Czechoslovakia alone. That they could possibly cure all that they claim to cure strains credulity.

At a place called Piestany, north of Bratislava, it seems to be another story. Here the atmosphere is more serious and clinical than it is touristic and the people who come to be helped are truly crippled with infirmities of age or broken by accidents of life. Twenty-five thousand a year come to Piestany, all with the faith that they will go away better off. The symbol of the place is a statue of a man breaking a crutch which he no longer needs.

If you are skeptical of what sulphur water or hot, slimey mud packs can do for arthritis or rheumatism or for the after-effects of orthopedic surgery, you can speak frankly with Dr. Oldrich Blaha who is the chief doctor at the sanitorium. He's been challenged before. Ask him: Isn't all this spa stuff just a myth, a form of quackery which holds out hope for a cure that doesn't exist? Dr. Blaha's answers are calm.

"It's true, not all the physicians of Europe will send their patients here. . . . It's true we don't know what rheumatism is and we don't know why our treatments work. . . . No, they don't work for everyone. . . . Yes, there is a purely psychological effect. . . . No, there is nothing miraculous about the water. We use it only because it is a convenient source of 700,000 gallons per day. It contains 150 milligrams of sulphur per litre and it comes out of the earth at 67 degrees Centigrade, which is very hot. . . . All we know is that we improve the mobility of people's joints through hydrotherapy, exercise and a restful environment. If there is a cure, it will come through drugs. In the meantime, we provide symptomatic relief. . . ."

There are 2200 beds in seven hotels at Piestany, 850 of them in three attractive, modern establishments built by the government. Czech citizens come here for three to four weeks of rest, recreation and treatment and pay little or nothing. Foreigners usually come for two weeks and pay a surprisingly low rate for room, board, recreation (mini-golf, tennis, water skiing, horseback riding, music festivals) and, of course, treatment. There is seldom a waiting list except in summer.

Recently, as many as 1000 Americans a year have been going to Piestany for care. Before they returned home, some of them went dancing for the first time in years. They weren't cured, but they felt better. Is there a difference?

◆ ◆ ◆

In the small villages of the High Tatras, Czech peasants still dance in colorful native costumes as they did a century ago. It is not a daily event, but on holidays and for weddings, dancing to the old music is still a favorite recreation. The Tatras are a small but rugged range of mountains in the northeast. It is a region steeped in tradition, Alpine in flavor, where the clear air is scented with woodsmoke the year round and the streets of small towns echo to the clump of young people striding in heavy climbing boots.

The Tatras were once considered remote for most tourists, but since the world ski championships for Nordic events were held here in 1970, the area is opening up fast—skiiers in winter; hikers, campers and nature lovers in other seasons. For a visitor coming from historic old Prague, Old Smokovec seems like that town in the fairy tale where Hungarian dukes came to hunt and vampires lived in the forests.

Indeed, the region of the Tatras is a national park where deer, chamois, bears, lynxes and wolves are protected. The central massif of mountains is about 17 miles from east to west and the highest peak is 8000 feet. Tourists fly to Poprad, the airport town of the Tatras, on CSA jets, then drive to the cluster of four towns called the "Smocovecs"—Old, New, Upper and Lower.

The 120-room Grand Hotel in Old Smocovec was built in the classic style of mountain resorts circa 1903 and has somehow survived 70 years of good times and bad. It has a threadbare gentility. Nearby, the 110-room Belleview, built in 1965 by the government, is the newest hotel. It is modern, functional and bland. It has a pool and a massage room. Thirty-four other, smaller hotels bring the total number of rooms in the region to 1200.

The most impressive evidence that the Czech government is serious about developing tourism in the Tatras is the new, 151-room Hotel Patria, now under construction and due to open in 1975. It is a striking piece of alpine-style architecture in a dramatic setting.

With the cost of skiing at French, Italian and Swiss resort areas rising every year, the Czechs hope to attract more visitors to their facilities in the Tatras—and to their fixed prices, which are hard to beat.

◆　◆　◆

The country that tourists come to see is often in between the places they stop to look at. For example, in Czechoslovakia, the open road itself. The country has an excellent network of highways, but, to an American, Czech driving habits seem appalling. The speed limit which is most universally observed is the car's maximum velocity just short of going off the road. There are very few police in rural areas. You are much more likely to get a ticket in the city. (When you do, the police officer tells you what your fine will be on the spot. You pay him cash, he gives you a receipt, salutes and says goodbye.)

In the country, cultivated farmland still seems to occupy a large part of the CSSR. Fat, brown cattle graze in rolling pastureland, big cabbages gleam like rows of blue-green cannonballs under irrigation sprays and plum trees are so heavy with purple fruit in the fall that their branches must be propped up with poles. There is a feeling of plenty.

Roadsides and small towns are often defaced with political graffiti in the form of large red posters bearing yellow lettering. They are put in place by the Party and are usually quotations from Lenin or Marx or exhortations to work harder for the triumph of socialism. Some are apparently condemnations of "imperialismu!" Cedok guides tactfully avoid translations.

War memorials in solid black granite with wreaths of bright red plastic flowers are sometimes the only spot of color in the gray little farm towns that crowd both sides of the highways.

At Lechovice, about 50 kilometers south of Brno, the road leads to a Kulturi Dum, the "culture house" of a collective farm. The large stone building could be a post office or a courthouse and appears out of place in the middle of farmland. This collective has been successful in recent years with sales of its packaged cheese and dairy products so it could afford to build its own culture house. It is used for meetings, concerts, banquets. It also provides a restaurant for the traveling public, the only one for miles around. The waiters and waitresses are quite properly dressed in black and white uniforms, but the dining room has more flies than a dairy barn. Lunch-of-the-day is usually goulash: three pieces of meat, some slices of hardboiled egg, onions and lots of chewy bread to dip in the gravy.

◆ ◆ ◆

Such are the peculiarities of air service in the CSSR that if you wish to travel from the Tatras to Brno, Czechoslovakia's second city, it is sometimes better to fly via Bratislava which is several hundred miles out of the way in the wrong direction. This itinerary will also expose the tourist to some revealing contrasts in aircraft. From Poprad to Bratislava, CSA flies a slick jet, the well-appointed Tupolev 134A. From Bratislava to Brno, some flights are made by an altogether quaint, spotlessly clean and surprisingly roomy Ilyushin 14, a twin-engine propeller plane of DC3 vintage with fabric-covered ailerons, overhead parcel racks of string mesh, genuine leather armrests and comfortable but nonreclining seats.

Upon arrival at Brno airport, the visitor can be snapped back to the realities of the Nato-vs-Warsaw Pact-world by the thunder of Mig fighter planes taking off on training flights, their roaring afterburners painting the evening sky with exclamation points of white flame. The Migs disappear over the old Gothic fortress of Spilberk where the Nazis had a guillotine for the execution of Czech patriots.

◆   ◆   ◆

No one questions Czech patriotism, but it has often been noted that when confronted with a superior force, the Czechs have not always chosen to be resistance fighters and martyrs. No significant Czech underground developed after Hitler took over the country in 1938; none appeared 30 years later when the Red armies moved against Dubcek. In the same decades, thousands of passionate Poles and Hungarians died fighting oppression of one brand or another, but the stolid Czechs have a tragic sense; they have learned to bend rather than break. This has earned them a reputation for having what one writer has called "flexible spines."

It was another Czech writer, Jaroslav Hasek, who, following World War I, created a sympathetic symbol of the infuriatingly passive Czech, a fictional private in the Austrian army named Schweik. In a brilliant comic novel titled *The Adventures of the*

Good Soldier Schweik, Hasek drew a character more real than life to most Czechs, a dumb, obedient victim of the bureaucratic system who, for all his innocence, usually managed to frustrate authority and drive his masters to despair.

During the Nazi occupation, the Czechs had a word, *svejkovina,* which meant "doing it Schweik's way," i.e., screw things up if you can, but don't get yourself in trouble. Like the G.I. word snafu, *svejkovina* found a thousand uses in conversation.

When the communists took over in Czechoslovakia in 1948, the works of Hasek and his contemporary, Kafka, were banned and Good Soldier Schweik went underground. Then, when Krushchev denounced Stalinism, Schweik returned. The government even rebuilt *U kalicha,* the tavern in Prague which Hasek frequented and which played a prominent part in the Schweik tales. Now Cedok encourages tourists to visit the once-proscribed place for a beer or a light meal. Schweik souvenirs are sold and the walls are decorated with cartoon illustrations from the Good Soldier's famous adventures.

Unfortunately, now that *U kalicha* is a state-owned enterprise, and the character of Schweik has been officially laundered, there is a sterile quality to the place. The food is only average, the atmosphere contrived. One suspects that the little soldier wouldn't think much of the present management, that his name is being used, but his free spirit is absent.

◆ ◆ ◆

The spirit of freedom is timid in Czechoslovakia. The three-day tourist, intent upon shopping and sightseeing, may never notice that Prague's newsstands carry nothing but communist newspapers and magazines. No *Time,* no *Paris Match,* no *Manchester Guardian,* no *Der Spiegel.* A young Czech will tell you that not even in the universities are western publications allowed to enter for study. She adds, "If we want to know what's really going on in the rest of the world, we sometimes go to the foreign airline offices or embassies. They often leave some western publications lying around their waiting rooms."

The spirit of fun is inhibited in Czechoslovakia. Irony has replaced humor. Fear often squelches laughter. The absurd is seen as possible.

Waiting at an airport, a camera-toting American aims a long lens out the window at nothing and jokes with his Cedok guide. "Come on, Jan, let's go photograph some Migs!"

But it's no joke and there are no smiles. Jan pretends not to hear.

The spirit of communication is guarded in Czechoslovakia. The cat has got somebody's tongue. For example, a conversation while strolling through the zoo in Bratislava:

"Where is Mr. Dubcek now?"

"He is here in Bratislava."

"What does he do?"

"He works for the government."

"What is his job?"

"Something in transportation."

"In the U.S. it has been written that he works in a garage."

"Perhaps. No one knows."

The spirit of security is strong in Czechoslovakia. On the road near a border crossing, an army truck passes and draws ahead, revealing its passengers in the rear, a half dozen soldiers, each holding the leash of a muzzled German shepherd. Animals and men look back at the following car in a tableau of suspicion.

"Where are they going with the dogs?"

"To duty."

"Who are they looking for?"

"Unauthorized travelers."

"Are there many of those?"

"Sometimes."

◆   ◆   ◆

The American travelers without passports got them back eventually. The little books with the Secretary of State's noble words on the first page caught up with the two tourists when they returned to Prague. A Cedok messenger brought them to the airport in a sealed envelope and solemnly handed them over. Now the Americans were no longer un-people. No more visits to police stations. Now they could register in a hotel, travel about, change currency—and cross the Czech frontier.

"I'm sorry, but this is where I must leave you," said the man from Cedok as they came to the last gate. There was a guard beyond. They said goodbye and the Americans passed by the guard on the way to their plane.

At that moment, the two little blue-green books acquired a new meaning.

CHAPTER 8
Takayama, a Secret Place

JAPAN, I HAD BEEN told, is a land of serene beauty, clear and pure as a note from a temple bell, contemplative as a haiku poem, peaceful as a garden at evening. So I was told. But in my early travels, I had seen only another sort of Japan —in Tokyo, the neon fireworks of the Ginza, the fun and games of Asakusa, the gaudy discount wonderland of Akihabara. At Nikko, I felt like one among a million pilgrims climbing the endless stone steps to Toshogu shrine. At Toba, I was one among a million schoolboys visiting the birthplace of cultured pearls. In Nagoya, I saw how millions of automobiles take shape in the crackling fire of the welders' torches; in Hamamatsu it was motorcycles; in Yokohama it was supertankers. In Osaka I was lost in the labyrinth of a huge railroad station that seemed a city in itself. I traveled the Tokaido via bullet trains, the truck-clogged highways via private car, and flew across vast estuaries in fast-skimming hydrofoils. In all my experience, Japan was speed, action, congestion, power—but serenity, no.

Then I found Takayama.

79

It is often said that this quaint, quiet city of 58,000 is the Japanese Williamsburg, or "a little Kyoto," a place where the past has been lovingly preserved, where one can see what old Japan was like prior to the Meiji Restoration.

"Oh, I envy you your visit there!" a Japanese friend in Tokyo exclaimed. "Takayama is a place where every Japanese wants to go once in his lifetime." (My only concern was that I would find each one of them there at the same time!)

But Takayama has a protection from crowds—its location in the high mountains of central Japan. You must go there deliberately, for although this town is almost the geographical center of Honshu, it is not a stopping off place between Japanese cities. Nor is it a resort town, religious retreat, health spa or center of commerce. Its temples are not the gilded palaces of Kyoto. Its restaurants are not the steak houses of Kobe. Its nightclubs are nonexistent.

One goes to Takayama, finally, in answer to a call. Come and see old Japan, it says. Come into the Hida mountains where time has slowed.

The route north from Nagoya is the Chuo line; the train is the Norikura express. In three hours or more it winds its way through heavily forested gorges, going ever deeper into the mountains, following wild, rocky riverbeds which could be in Idaho or Switzerland. It is big timber country; logs await the sawmills and small furniture factories use the lumber. For more than a thousand years, Japan's best carpenters have come from the Hida region and yew tree carving is something boys learn at an early age. "The people here love wood," you are told.

The city lives in a valley between mountains, and when the sun sets in October or April, the snowcapped peaks of the Japan Alps stand like a towering, golden fence around Takayama.

The Miyagawa River comes down from the mountains and

runs through the town and in the shadow of bridges, red carp and trout and sweetfish prowl the clear water. When deep winter comes to Takayama, the river freezes and the fish sleep and the snows move down from the mountains and muffle the town, and children coast on sleds with wooden runners.

A visitor to Takayama is accepted, but never solicited. Last year, thousands of Japanese, but only 148 foreign tourists went there. There are a dozen hotels and ryokans, none of them large, and a new people's lodging with 26 rooms. There are a few taxis around the railroad station. But the best way to see much of Takayama is on foot, for it is a small town, its historical center no larger than a New England village. Its citizens will welcome you in their most genuine way—by ignoring you. The people of the region are said to have a native poise that is unique. I remembered my small-town Massachusetts upbringing and how a few words could sometimes be given more meaning than many.

For over 300 years, one of Takayama's distinguishing customs has been the flower and vegetable market which sets up each morning like a colorful medieval campsite along one side of the lively river. Farmers' wives arrive shortly after sunup with handcarts and bicycles and bamboo baskets overladen with flowers, vegetables, mushrooms, nuts and fruits. They display their products in boxes and on mats for several blocks along the small street, sometimes also erecting fabric-covered lean-to's overhead to filter the sun.

By nine, the market is a busy yet graceful scene. There are no weighing scales, no price tags, no cries of vendors, nor any sign of haggling. Nature's whole palette of colors is assembled and arrayed: golden chrysanthemums wrapped in a twist of newspaper; red rooted vegetables tied in bunches, moist brown earth still clinging to them; dark, polished eggplant and yellow-white cabbages all in a row.

The housewives of Takayama move along the stalls by the river wearing white aprons over heavy kimonos, their hair drawn back in sleek black buns, their arms accumulating packages as they go. They greet friends among the farmers' wives who squat among the boxes and chatter. *Asaichi,* the morning market, is a colorful performance, a ritual in which buyers and sellers alike seem to know their roles from centuries of practice and tradition.

The taste of food in Takayama is noted for its clarity, for the clean definition of its flavors, a benefit said to be derived from clean air and pure water at 1800 feet elevation. So, be praised, is the sake also benefitted. It is brewed with almost sacramental care from Hida rice and mountain waters and sold by several makers in town. Their brand names would be known as far away as Tokyo, but their distilleries are unmarked by signs or advertising. Look for a house where a great cinnamon-colored ball, big as a wagon wheel, hangs by the door. This *sugitama* is made from layer on layer of cedar leaves, sculpted into a sphere. It is the discreet and traditional symbol of a sake maker.

Step in the open door and you will find a small shop where bottles are displayed—shos and gos, stonewear or glass, packed and labeled with pride, "Made in Hida-Takayama, Japan." The breath of the sake hangs in the air of the house, alerting your nostrils with pleasure.

Takayama has two great festivals every year in April and October. They are dedicated to planting and harvesting, but they are also occasions for the town to parade its greatest treasures, a collection of massive floats, each taller than the average house, rich with carvings, gilt and lacquer and brilliantly illuminated at night with lanterns. Eleven of these ancient, Edo-period masterpieces can be seen year round in a special museum in town.

True to its "Williamsburg" reputation, there are also other small museums in Takayama which display collections of religious valuables, lacquerware, traditional Japanese wooden toys, ancient armor and old tools and implements of the Hida region.

But Takayama's heritage is not only kept behind glass in museums. Some of its old streets preserve the look of centuries, unmarred by utility poles and wires, closed to automobile traffic, sanctuaries of the past where the unpainted wood of old lattice-front houses has aged to rich brown and the stone steps at doorways are worn smooth by the generations.

Many of Takayama's old mansions are still the residences of tradesman families; a few have been opened to the public as living examples of earlier ages. The interior of the 100-year-old Kusakabes' house displays huge foot-square beams, perfectly fitted, a tribute to the woodworking skills of Hida-region builders. The 1781 Hirata House is furnished with screens, lanterns and other outstanding examples of Edo-period decor.

An altogether different sort of architecture can be seen a short distance from town in the foothills of Mt. Matsukura where a number of unique, four-story gassho-zukuri houses have been reconstructed in a typical Hida village. The name of these huge, steep-roofed farmhouses derives from "putting hands together" as in prayer. They sometimes sheltered as many as 50 people from three or four families, a sort of 19th Century communal experiment known as *dai kazoku sai* or "big family system." In the harsh winters of the Hida, as heavy snows slid from the thick susuki-grass thatch of the roofs, open fires heated these big dormitory-like houses from the ground floor up, the smoke being allowed to rise through the entire building and escape from the peaks of the roof.

Of course, what Japanese city would be complete without its

temples and shrines? Takayama, a castle town in feudal times, also has its share of ancient holy places—16 or more—but in this unusual city, where the tradesman and the artisan and the farmer have all left such distinct traces of their cultures, where antiquity is a daily companion, traditional places of worship, however old or famous, can be taken for granted.

Within the 1200-year-old Hida Kokubunji temple, near the center of Takayama, a sitting image of Yakushi and a standing image of Kannon, both carved from wood, are classified as important cultural properties of Japan. Nearby, in a small park, the temple's three-story pagoda and an ancient ginko tree have become part of a children's playground. Little ones in school uniforms come there with their teachers for morning recess and, in the afternoon, older boys, wearing baseball jackets lettered with the names *Giants* and *Hawks,* sometimes loosen up their pitching arms in the shadow of history.

CHAPTER 9
Looking for a Hideaway in Greece

IT WAS A BRIGHT young March day and although the whole idea seemed a bit odd, I was about to go shopping for real estate in the Greek islands. I should have been the first to admit that I had no particular qualifications for this adventure other than (1) having been through the experience of buying a couple of houses in suburban Connecticut, and (2) having taken a brief tourist's tour around Mykonos and its windmills a few years earlier. The first experience had left me with the feeling that I would prefer never to deal with real estate agents again. The second made me wish that I might return to Mykonos and the beautiful Aegean, the sooner the better.

Now I was on the docks at Piraeus, the *Never On Sunday* town, looking for a boat named *Oia* (Eee-a) which I had been assured would sail for Syros at 8:45 A.M. Piraeus, which is only a 20-minute cab ride from Athens, is a small, noisy port where ships of all sorts and sizes are tied up at the piers with their winches rattling and booms reaching, some of them just arrived, some preparing to sail, a few with their names clearly marked, but most of them painted a uniform white and looking as much alike to a stranger as trolley cars in a foreign city.

The scheme which had brought me here had somehow been hatched at a luncheon in New York weeks earlier. A magazine editor I knew had said he'd be interested in an article about places where people could run away and hide—and maybe buy a little house for a song. Positano. Baja. Durban. The Seychelles. That sort of thing.

"How about Mykonos?" I had suggested—and here I was in Greece.

My cab driver found *Oia* at last after much cruising up and down the quai and shouting many questions in Greek. The ship was snugged up tight to a pier with her cargo hatches open, a nice looking vessel with a rakish bow, lots of polished brass, a single smoke stack, a radar turning briskly at her masthead and the blue and white Greek flag hanging limply at the stern. A man I took to be the captain was out on the bridge making commanding gestures, the gold braid on his blue uniform sleeves gleaming as he waved his arms. He seemed to be telling everyone to go away, including me and my cab.

"The captain is saying he will not sail today because of a technical inspection of the ship," my driver explained.

It is one of the authentic charms of Greece that schedule changes are never announced until they happen.

"You go to Syros tomorrow instead?" my driver asked.

"No," I said, annoyed, "I go to Syros *today.*"

"Okay, we look for another boat."

That there might be another boat was something that had never occurred to me.

"Oh, sure," said the cabbie in his best American, "plenty boats. I think it is better you don't go on *Oia* anyway. Captain not telling the truth. No inspection. Ship has bent propeller.

Very bad. Make ship shake all over. You no like. We find another."

I agreed.

Next we found *Elli,* a somewhat bigger and less graceful craft but with healthy propellers and sailing for Syros at 11 A.M. I paid off my helpful cabbie, bought tickets from *Elli's* purser who had a folding table set up on the dock and went aboard. No reservations necessary, just hoist your own bag across the gangway and then look for Spiros Maranakis, the first class steward. When I explained the problem with *Oia,* Maranakis just smiled knowingly.

"Not propellers," he said, shaking his head and putting on a sly look. "Seas sometimes too rough for *Oia* in March. *Oia* is a summer boat, likes smooth sailing."

I acknowledged this information with a nod, as if I both believed and understood.

◆ ◆ ◆

If you approach the Aegean ferry services with an easy and, above all, flexible spirit, they are some of the greatest bargain cruises anywhere in the world. The fares have increased every time I go back, but indeed they could double or triple and still be a bargain. Not every travel agent will take the trouble—or is it the risk?—to book clients on these inter-island boats, however, because the schedules are not only subject to whimsical changes from time to time, but because understanding how the system works can be complicated. For example, there are a dozen or more boats (*Marilena, Knossos, Sofia, Adonis, Mario, Leto,* etc.) crisscrossing and circling the islands of the Aegean. Most sail from Piraeus on 3- to 5-day schedules and return; a few merely move among the islands, touching at some once a week and at others only on certain days. If you are just freelance touring, it's quite possible to get stuck on a particular island for a day or two longer than you planned. The boat you were expecting may develop, say, propeller trouble and just not show up. Shipping agents on the islands are no help. They tend to have several other jobs, such as cutting hair or repairing motorcycles, and are usually indifferent to passengers' problems. No boat today, they will tell you. Tomorrow, maybe. And tomorrow, of course, one does arrive. What were you worrying about?

◆   ◆   ◆

Elli sailed at 11 and shortly thereafter Steward Maranakis found me reading in the lounge. A drink before lunch? Yes, a Metaxa sour, 20 cents in those days, would be fine. The menu promised chicken, lamb or veal steak, Greek salad (chunks of white goat cheese, cucumbers, tomatoes and ripe olives in oil), Domestica wine and bakalava with coffee. $1.40—again, in those days.

There were only a few other off-season passengers in the dining room. We watched small, barren islands pass close by as *Elli* headed for the open sea. As we left land behind, I could see the temple standing high on Sounian's bluff, like a marble offering on nature's own altar.

"Classic house on high ground," I thought. "Pretty view, low taxes, great possibilities, but needs work," I continued facetiously. What kind of real estate discoveries would I really make in the islands? Was this all an absurd idea anyway?

◆   ◆   ◆

We arrived at Syros about 4 P.M., gliding into the pocket of the harbor as smoothly as a billiard ball. I carried my bags down *Elli*'s steep gangplank and then just across the street to the only hotel on the island, the Hermes. After registering and being shown to a spacious $3.50 room with a balcony overlooking the sea (but no hot water; the off-season has some disadvantages too) I began to explore my first island on foot. Surely there would be a real estate office somewhere!

Syros rises from the sea at a steep angle. The town is built on the 45 degree slopes of two conical peaks, one of them crowned with a cathedral. Up and down traffic, on foot or by donkey, is via stairs, not streets. Everything seems neat, clean, compact and poor. A few souvenir shops and tavernas face the harbor and several candy stores sell the island specialty, nougat. There is a main square in the center of the town and an imposing if inappropriate government building with a long flight of marble steps leading up to the door. This looked like a place where I might learn something about the local real estate situation.

Inside, I moved down a dark hall until I came to a courtroom where a trial was in progress. Someone had been robbed or raped, I couldn't tell which. Greeks often sound as if they are angry with each other in just normal conversation; in court they are even more vehement.

Beyond the courtroom, at the end of the hall, I came to an office, dimly lit, where a middle aged man worked at a desk surrounded by file cabinets. Mr. George Lambis was a clerk of the court. I introduced myself and in simple English phrases told him I wanted to know how much a house might cost on Syros, how much land cost, and who should I see about doing this sort of business?

Lambis got up from his desk and tossed a scrap of firewood into a small sheetmetal stove in the corner of the office. He was a man in his fifties with gray hair, steel frame glasses, a gray sweater over his vest. His hands were stained with the purple ink of rubber stamps. The stove crackled but gave no heat.

"There is a man named Roussos who knows about this," said Lambis. "He lives in another village on the island, but he comes here every morning to buy groceries. If you will come back

tomorrow between 8 and 9, I will find him for you." I said I
would.

Evening was approaching. Smoke was rising from the chim-
neys of houses. On the way back to the hotel, I stopped at the
post office to ask the postmaster what he knew about Roussos
the real estate man. He said he didn't know Roussos. In fact,
he said after consulting his Greek-English dictionary, there
"was not no body" in that line of work on this island. "However," he added, "my name is Steve Toledis and I can help
you." He said he knew all about land and prices. He said I
would have to pay 1000 drachmas for a square meter of land
in town.

I said that sounded like a lot of money, $33 for every 9 square
feet.

"Don't worry about the price," said the postmaster. "There
isn't any land for sale in town anyway."

I headed back along the harbor toward the Hermes. A boat
named *Mario* had docked during the afternoon. Now it was
ablaze with harbor lights, festive as a Christmas tree.

When I picked up my room key at the hotel, the young man
at the desk said there would be no dinner in the dining room
tonight because the stove was broken. Perhaps it is too early in
the season, I thought. After all, there was no hot water either.
Perhaps "broken" meant "too early."

Later, a young man of the hotel escorted me wordlessly
through the streets of the harbor front to a taverna whose
proprietor seemed to know all about the broken stove at the
Hermes and said he was giving me dinner without charge. He
shrugged and smiled and wiped his hands on his apron and said
he was sorry. Just choose anything I wanted. He fixed a great
meal.

The next morning the tiny stove in Lambis' office was still

crackling and still giving no heat. Three men were there, stand-ing awkwardly, caps in hand, apparently waiting for the Ameri-can who said he wished to buy land. One of them was Roussos himself, a second, younger man was Roussos' son, Andreas. The third was Nicholas Daras who once lived on East 34th Street in New York and worked as a cook in a Catskill's hotel.

The four of us walked across the square to a taverna for coffee. Morning loiterers watched us as if they knew that An-dreas Roussos was about to have an important discussion with a rich American about buying land on Syros.

Young Roussos started the conversation by saying that he was a merchant seaman and had once made port in San Fran-cisco where he took a bus for New York. He said the five-day land journey had come as a surprise to him. He thought New York was just a few hours away at most. Everyone around the table laughed at this and the atmosphere relaxed. Now we were all friends. More coffee.

Roussos Sr. wore his cap, a dark shirt buttoned at the neck, no tie, a suit jacket and a gray topcoat. He said he ran a grocery store in the country. He took a small notebook from an inside coat pocket. In it were listed various parcels of land which he said were for sale. There was a 4-room house on a quarter acre just out of town. The price was 250,000 drachmas, less than $9000. Also, in the town of Vari nearby there was a new 5-room house on six hectares (about an acre and a half) with fruit trees. Also for $9000.

But how much would it cost, I asked, to buy a piece of land near the sea and build my own 2-bedroom house on it? I was thinking of my magazine editor back in New York and what he was looking for.

Three heads all swiveled slowly, back and forth. Very expen-sive. With plumbing and electricity? Of course, I said. Well, probably at least 300,000 drachs—$10,000. But mind you, Roussos said, prices are going up and soon such a place may cost $12,000. Indeed.

◆ ◆ ◆

The next day it was *Oia* which turned up at Syros to take me on to Santorini. As I came aboard, I asked the captain if the technical inspection at Piraeus had gone well. He looked at me curiously and said the problem wasn't a technical inspection but an order from the port director not to sail.

I went forward on the boat deck, took off my shirt and soaked up some March sun. I heard the crew casting off lines and soon the gentle movement of the ship underway lulled me to sleep.

By sunset the weather turned bad and we didn't reach Santorini until nearly midnight. Overhead, low, black clouds torn ragged by the storm, raced wildly across the face of a full moon. In this strange, on-again, off-again light, the island loomed ahead like a black iceberg floating on a silver sea. Nowhere on this dark shape could I see even a pinpoint of light.

Because the harbor of Santorini is the 1500-foot-deep crater of a once great volcano, ships can not anchor, but heave-to while small boats from the island come alongside to exchange passengers and cargo. They announced their presence this night with bobbing lights on the water and diesel engines which popped loudly over the sounds of the waves. There were two of them standing off, waiting for permission to move alongside *Oia*'s open hatches.

As passengers and crewmembers waited to step out into the small boats, a scene developed which looked like old pictures of immigrants at Ellis Island. We were all jammed into a narrow passageway together: people, animals, cheeses, furniture, poultry, bags of mail, bottles of wine, baby carriages, automobile batteries, brass beds, a new Japanese motorcycle, flagpoles and many large bundles carefully sewed tight in cloth wrappings.

A bent little man approached me out of the melee and identified himself as "Moolie." He touched his chest with a forefinger as he said the name. He indicated that I was in his care. A good thing too, I thought.

As it turned out, Moolie seemed to be in charge of many things, including some special mail which he stuffed up under his sweater. After about 15 minutes of chaos, during which *Oia*'s captain, gold braid and all, assisted in shoving a large sofa with sagging springs out into one of the small boats, Moolie indicated it was time for me to leave. *Oia,* her harbor lights ablaze, dwindled astern our small boat as we put-putted in toward the dark island.

Everything about Santorini has been shaped by the cataclysmic event which tore through the earth's crust there about 1500 B.C. The principal town, Thera, is perched on the rim of the ex-volcano, 900 dizzying feet above the place where I stepped out of the boat with Moolie. There was now only one way to get from the boat to the town—and that's why Moolie is called Moolie: he is a mule keeper and everyone who is going up to Thera tonight pays him 85 cents for a ride up the cliff road on one of his animals. My bags and camera gear went on the back of one donkey and I mounted another. Moolie gave the creatures a sound slap on the rumps and up we went along a steep, switchback road which the animals seemed to know well enough, but which seemed both dark and precarious to me.

With Moolie somewhere behind and only the unknown ahead, I turned 90 degrees on the donkey's back and looked down on the strange harbor where islands of undulating pumice floated on the surface like small white rugs gleaming in the occasional moonlight, a ghostly reminder of the disaster 3400 years ago. *Oia* was already sailing away.

Clattering down the road came fresh reinforcements of mules and donkeys, adroitly avoiding the upcoming line of traffic, making their way to the harbor unescorted in the darkness, small brass bells around their necks jingling in unison, like an obedient band of children all racing each other to school.

There are only two or three hotels on Santorini, but it is the 36-room Atlantis that dominates the skyline at the edge of the cliff and it was there that my animals brought me when we had finally negotiated the 586 cobbled steps of the zig-zag road. The Atlantis, I would soon learn, was built in 1955 by Emmanuel Vazeos. He came out at the sound of my donkey's hooves and welcomed me to his hotel. He also carried in my bags, remarking as he led the way that the boat was very late tonight. He added that he was sorry there would be no heat in the room just now because the boiler was broken. He said I could get hot water for washing from the kitchen if I would bring down a pail.

In morning light, with the storm still blowing and the wind cold, there was something weird about Santorini—and the Atlantis. I soon deduced that I was the only guest. My footsteps echoed along the marble halls. Vazeos had canaries in hanging cages in the large, draughty lobby. They accompanied the cry of the wind with a mad chorus of singing. Long vines whose roots originated in great amphora-shaped pots on the stair landings wound their way along the corridor walls, passing over doorways, clinging to anything provided, penetrating down dark halls as if in search of some special nourishment.

The dining room of the Atlantis appeared to seat about 60, but in March, if you were the only guest, it seemed a curious charade to see all the tables set and waiting for guests who would not come.

Somewhere in the kitchen there was an unseen cook who

prepared dorado fish with skill and once I saw a young chambermaid upstairs. In the dining room, Vazeos sat at an old flat-top desk, keeping his accounts and watching me eat. Sometimes he made a little conversation.

"In 1956, when we had the last earthquake," he said once, "this dining room was the morgue. We had 76 dead then. All of them here on the marble floor.

"The old volcano isn't quite finished yet, you see . . ."

Like Pompeii, Santorini is a time capsule, a place where archaeologists dig through a mantle of volcanic ash hundreds of feet deep to discover a well-preserved world of 1500 B.C.

"Who should I see if I wanted to buy some land on this island?" I asked Vazeos.

"You would see me," he said, taking this as an invitation to come and sit with me at breakfast. "I do everything for my guests. I have been in the hotel business since I was 12, here and in Egypt. I built this place the year before the earthquake. Two thousand homes in Santorini were destroyed, but the hotel stood. We had tremors every day for a month."

I pulled the thick skin from my Naxos orange, imported to arid Santorini from the largest and lushest of the Cyclades. Vazeos stirred his coffee.

"If you want to buy land here, I can arrange it," he said. "I charge you no commission. I paid only $10,000 for the 1200 square meters of land to build this hotel. Today you can still buy 200 to 300 square meters of land here for $1000 and you can build a new house on it for another $2000."

The 1956 earthquake left ruins all over Santorini which still look like black, unfilled cavities. Some occupy sites of land with spectacular views of the volcano-harbor. One was being restored by a French investor who paid $5000 for the ruin and a small piece of land clinging to Santorini's dramatic precipice.

With the investment of another $5000 he would build a house with a view that Onassis himself would have envied.

Santorini casts a spell: excavations which have unearthed an ancient civilization; 2000 mules and donkeys, many of them roaming free; hundreds of acres of runty grape vines, their roots running deep into the volcanic ash. Santorini wine costs 20 cents a bottle—and you can rent a donkey all day for a dollar.

After a few days of exploring and suffering the strange chill of the Atlantis (the broken boiler never was fixed) it was old friend *Elli* which took me away from Santorini's towering cliffs, their sides burned red, black and gold by the scourging of primeval fires. I felt a tug. I could imagine a great $5000 house on a cliff . . .

Now I was headed for Mykonos.

♦ ♦ ♦

In 1967, I had met a man named Constantine Zouganelis on Mykonos. Unlike Roussos and Vazeos, Zouganelis was a *bona fide* real estate agent with an office and a sign and all. He was also the port director, operator of a night club called the Dive Inn, shipping agent and boarding house keeper. As my ship eased into the picture book harbor for my second visit to the island, I hoped I would find Zouganelis again.

Mykonos is *the* stereotype Greek island, complete with fishermen mending their nets, windmills turning in the sharp sea breeze, white-washed houses, lean cats dozing on geranium-decked balconies, boats of all shapes and colors, narrow stone-paved streets and the air seasoned overall with the rich smells of taverna cooking. In March, the gift shops bulged with fresh stocks of colorful knitwear, rugs and other hand woven goods which the islanders had produced over the winter for sale to an invasion of summer visitors. One of the brightest of these shops caught my eye as I came ashore. A chic young woman greeted me as I entered.

"Do you know a man named Zouganelis who used to be in the real estate business here?" I asked.

"You came to the right place," she said without a trace of surprise. "He is my husband."

Would he be around the store soon, I asked, hardly believing my good luck. Yes, she said, perhaps later, about six. "You see," the woman explained, "my husband is a very busy man these days. He is the new mayor of the island."

We met the next morning at the mayor's office, a quaint old room with creaking wood floors and home-made furniture on the second floor of the town hall. French doors opened onto a balcony which overlooked the harbor. Reflections of morning light dappled the room; large framed portraits of previous mayors looked down from the walls.

"Do you remember those house lots you showed me in 1967?" I asked. "I suppose they've all been snapped up by movie stars by now."

"Not at all," Zouganelis said. "You mean that nice land by the sea at Ayi Yianni? It is still there—and the price would still be about the same, say $2500 for half an acre."

His Honor was interrupted several times with official matters while we talked. It was a holiday and within the hour he would join the island school children and local militia and the patriarchs of the church in laying a wreath. He was dressed for the occasion in a black suit, white shirt, dark tie. Several military medals made a colorful array on his chest. He says he is somewhat of a hero to his islanders because in World War II he and an older brother served in Greek intelligence. The Germans caught the brother and executed him as a spy.

Mykonos hadn't changed much since 1967. You could still rent a room for 75 cents and have a good meal at Maria's taverna for $1.50. There was one movie house and several clubs which featured bouzouki and Greek folk songs at night and bacon-and-eggs breakfasts for the American kids in the morning. There were more boats in the harbor now, handsome, broad-beamed *caiques* of all sizes. For a few drachs it would not be hard to find a skipper of one of these who would take a visitor over to Delos—in Greek mythology, the birthplace of Apollo —or even to nearby Tinos.

And there was still the land for sale, and houses too. A few thousand would get you started. Your house, new or old, would have to be painted white according to tradition, of course, with a door preferably blue, the blue of the Greek flag.

You wouldn't need a car, a motor scooter would do, and you wouldn't need a pool because you can swim and snorkel in gin-clear water all along any Aegean beach. You could quit worrying about cholesterol on Mykonos—there's no fatty beef on the taverna menus and butter and eggs are scarce.

You probably wouldn't miss people or feel cut off from the world because thousands of foreign visitors come to the islands every summer and some of them look spectacular in bikinis.

The wine is good, if you stay away from the resinated variety and the fish is always this-morning fresh.

There's no Walter Cronkite or *Wall Street Journal,* of course, but then, that's one of the best reasons for the Aegean Sea.

CHAPTER 10
"KL" and Other Places

THE BIG Sikorsky helicopter was hot as a tin-roof shack under the tropical sun. Two thousand feet below, the gray-green China Sea sparkled. Overhead, the rotor whacked and thudded, vibrating the whole machine like an overpowered hot rod. It would take an hour to get where we were going, they said, an hour to fly 120 miles from the east coast of Malaysia on a line toward the Mekong Delta. But we weren't going to Viet Nam. We weren't going to any *place*. We were looking for a big iron thing on the sea below. I knew what it would look like: a leviathan standing on four colossal legs implanted on the ocean floor. It was not a vessel, not an island. More like a lunar module—$10 million worth of functional hardware; ugly, yet curiously adapted to its environment, a precarious perch on which men lived and worked.

The thing had a name, *North Star,* and a purpose: to explore for offshore oil.

"How soon will we see it?" I asked the pilot above the racket.

He just pointed ahead. I could see nothing. No boats, no

99

land, no waves or wakes disturbing the calm green of the water. Nothing floating, nothing flying—but us. Just an empty sea under a midday sun. Nevertheless, somewhere ahead was *North Star.* The pilot knew where; he'd made this trip a hundred times or more.

We had come from a place called Kuala Trengannu, a Malay town that probably never saw a helicopter before 1969. That's when men started looking for oil on the sea bottom east of Malaysia. Nobody knows how much oil is there, but it has been found in nearby Sumatra, Brunei and Indonesia. There may be more offshore Malaysia.

Long before the world became preoccupied with oil, Malaysia used to be Malaya, as British as Somerset Maugham from 1826 to World War II. The Japanese invaded in 1942 and remained until 1945. After the war, the Federation of Malaya had British support until final independence was granted in 1957.

I'd crammed this much information about the place before flying up from Singapore to do a story on the oil prospecting. I knew there was also tin and rubber in Malaysia—and shadow plays and batik fabrics and, according to my itinerary, a hotel called the Federal in a city called Kuala Lumpur. I liked the sound of that name. Kuala Lumpur. What did it mean? What would it be like?

❖ ❖ ❖

"We hope very much to increase our travel industry in the next few years," the Minister of Tourism was saying while a half dozen beautiful women in ornate Malay costumes danced to the music of chelempong bells and gendang drums. We were dining at a club called The Hut, on the outskirts of Kuala Lumpur. Someone had already whispered that the Minister was a silent partner in the enterprise. He was a man in his fifties, dark skinned, soft spoken, courtly in his manners. He wore the small black hat made famous by Sukarno of Indonesia and a richly colored batik shirt with a high collar.

"Hong Kong has two million tourists a year," he said, going into the official government spiel. "Singapore's tourism is rising. So why should we not expect to share in the growth of this area?"

Why not indeed, I said politely. I was noticing that the Minister kept his eye on one of the dancers while we talked. He smiled intimately at her whenever she passed close to our table and even in the graceful ritual of the dance, I thought she seemed to acknowledge the attention.

"We took a survey of our foreign visitors last year," the Minister said, explaining with practiced Madison Avenue phraseology why the results were certainly valid. "A very large percentage of our guests were happy with their visit here, we are sure of that. Of course, there were a few who said they did not find enough to do. And some said the found the weather too hot."

We were eating satay, cubes of beef grilled on thin bamboo sticks over a charcoal fire and then dipped into a sauce made from chili peppers and peanuts. The beer was cold, but the air conditioning only puffed through the room like an occasional breeze through a screen door. The dancers seemed detached from the heat, their bodies turning in practiced movements, their exotic eyes heavy with shadow, their hands fluttering in a secret sign language.

"Will you be here long?" the Minister asked.

"Only a few days," I said.

"That's a pity," he replied. "You must let us help you see the country."

I thanked him for the offer. The dancers had just finished a number called Harvest Festival and the drums and bells gave way to applause and then to recorded Western music for dancing. Several of the women, including the object of the minister's attention, came to our table with hands outstretched in an invitation to dance. Their faces, close up, were meticulously painted masks, as strange and exciting to a traveler as his first close up look at a new country—one where tourism is still an innocent ambition, not an old profession.

◆   ◆   ◆

North Star stood in 260 feet of water, a giant up to its knees. I could see it through the plexiglass nose of the helicopter. It grew into a lattice work of steel, like the exposed superstructure of a sunken ship. It seemed small and bristling; an unlikely looking place to land a big bird with whirling wings.

The rig looked more hospitable as we came nearer. It acquired color, too: great black legs, a white superstructure, splashes of rust, red life rafts and a yellow bulls-eye painted on a rectangular shelf cantilevered off one end. The Sikorsky hovered over this for a moment, then bumped down. There was nothing around the three sides of this breadboard but a clean 90-foot drop to the China Sea.

"China Sea" is an evocative phrase. I smell joss and hemp and see old junks with stained sails running ahead of a typhoon. But this day I heard a man say "Welcome aboard" in the broad twang of the American southwest. Big John, they called him, a petroleum engineer from Texas, a huge man in a faded coverall and a shiny hard hat. "Come in where it's cool," he said, standing in a doorway.

Inside was like a ship: corridors, staterooms, offices, all bright enamel paint and orderly. A distant hum of air conditioning and winches vibrated through the steel frame of this ship, but there was no movement of the deck underfoot. *North Star*'s giant feet were sunk 30 feet into the slime of the sea bottom.

"She quivers a little in a storm, but that's all we ever feel," Big John observed. There was a double-deck bunk in his office, a small desk, a couple of chairs, two portholes. Two other men squeezed through the door behind me.

"Like you to meet Cal," said Big John. "He's our tool pusher."

"Howdy," said Cal and there was no mistaking Oklahoma.

"You work for the oil company, Cal?" I asked.

"Not for us," said Big John. "His company owns *North Star*. They're under contract to drill this well. But next week they're going to haul out of here and go drill for somebody else off Thailand."

Back in Kuala Lumpur, a man had told me, "That *North Star* will never find oil for anybody. It's jinxed. It drilled in the North Sea in 1969 and found nothing. Then a big Japanese tug was hired to bring it out here. The tow took 5½ months—at 2 knots!"

♦ ♦ ♦

You begin to call Kuala Lumpur "KL" on your second day because everybody else does. It is friendly shorthand for a likeable place. KL is not a teeming Asian city; fewer than a million people live and work there. Sixty percent of these are Chinese, 20 percent Indian and 15 percent Malay—a population mix that doesn't exist out in Malaysia's rural areas where Malays are a majority.

The capital city is a clean, attractive place, neither Oriental nor Eastern in flavor. Old Moorish architecture blends with an exciting array of the most modern buildings in Asia and the streets swarm with cars, motor scooters, taxis, trishaws and pickup trucks. School children wear neat, well-kept uniforms and beautiful Asian women in sarongs, mini skirts or the flowing aodais of Indo-China, stroll under colorful parasols.

The men still play cricket in front of the Royal Selangor Golf Club at the heart of the city—Brits, Indians, Malays and Chinese, all in crisp whites, all playing the old Colonial game together in a new Third World atmosphere.

At the center of the city, the baroque Jame mosque of another era contrasts sharply with a new, $3 million, white marble National Mosque not far away. The architecture of the national parliament buildings reminds visitors of the U.S. Air Force Academy in Colorado and the National Monument is a heroic statue in bronze by the same artist who created the Iwo Jima Memorial in Washington. In the colonnade which surrounds the sculpture are displayed the proud old unit emblems from a British heritage: "King's African Rifles . . . Strike to Defend . . . The Sun Never Sets . . . Eternal Vigilance . . ."

On the outskirts of Kuala Lumpur there are plush residential districts, one called U.K. Heights, another known as Kenny Hills. Handsome houses surrounded by well-landscaped grounds cling to steep hillsides and look down on the city below. These establishments are kept tidy by $40-a-month gardeners and $50-a-month live-in maids. There is more than a touch of irony in a young Malaysian's words when he says, "Yes, Europeans like to have their houses looking down on others . . ."

But Europeans weren't the only ones. Following Malaysia's independence from Britain, these elite suburbs were the object of a curious new land rush. "The rich Chinese Tin Daddies and Rubber Daddies fought to see who would take over the old English mansions," your Malasian friend tells you. "Some fantastic prices were paid."

Then the Chinese were looking down the hill at the Malays.

Tin Daddies and Rubber Daddies. In Malaysia's *laissez faire* colonial past, they were the economic powers. In those days it didn't take a $10 million piece of equipment like *North Star* to find wealth. It could be done with a shovel. In fact, if it were not for an expedition of Chinese tin prospectors who camped at the confluence of the Klang and Gombak rivers about a century ago, Kuala Lumpur (the name means "muddy river mouth") might not even exist today.

◆ ◆ ◆

"Hey," said Big John, reaching for the other man in the room, "want you to meet our own Chink!"

The ethnic slur shocked my ears until I saw the big Texan slip his arm around the shoulders of a small young man in the white coveralls of a technician. We were introduced.

"Are you Malaysian?" I asked. I wasn't sure of his name.

"He's no Malay!" roared Big John. "I told you: he's a Chink!" Laughter and cameraderie; rough talk and gentle behavior. These were oil men above all; they had no time for racisim except to joke about it. Ashore, in racially troubled Malaysia, it would be another story. The Constitution prohibits public discussions of racial subjects ever since Chinese and Malays went on an orgy of killing a few years ago. But on *North Star* it didn't matter where a man was from. Big John and Cal and the young Chinese with a degree in petroleum engineering and 90 other men aboard had just drilled a well together, hadn't they? Nine thousand, two hundred twenty feet deep.

"Find any oil?"

"We wouldn't tell you if we did!" Then a good natured laugh to cover. Oil exploration is a cagey business—anywhere, anytime. It is especially so in Southeast Asia. Some experts have called it one of the hottest potential areas in the world. Several big American companies are there. So are the English, French, Italians, Japanese, Australians and Germans. All probing the ancient sediment which flowed out from Asian rivers millions of years ago. The kind of stuff that sometimes makes oil.

"We've found some gas," Big John said, dropping the kidding. "As a matter of fact, we almost didn't let you land that chopper out here today because we're going to have to flow the well. Come on outside and I'll show you what I mean."

We went out into the heat. Amidships, *North Star* resembled a freighter in port—a jumble of deck machinery, hoses, wires, pipes, cables, and looming over all at the stern was the derrick. I had been told that it cost $30,000 a day to run a rig like this, that you could spend 100 days or more drilling a well and still find nothing.

"But you never know what may be just two inches below the spot where you *stop* drilling," the oil executive back in KL had said with a quizzical smile and a shrug. Then he swept his hand across a large map.

"We have this 28,000 square mile concession off the east coast. It's a license to look for oil from the Malaysian government. It's an area bigger than Maine. We've drilled 12 wells there since 1969, 12 pinpricks on the ocean floor, that's all they are. We've found some gas and some very minor shows of oil, but nothing that gives us much optimism."

The oil man, a Swiss engineer, had the detachment of a scientist. The glamor and excitement of probing deep for the earth's greatest treasure did not faze him. "Our term of life here is uncertain," he said matter-of-factly. "If we don't find anything, we'll have to move on and spend our money somewhere else."

A lot of money is involved. Drilling 12 peepholes into a 28,000-square-mile mystery costs $2 to $3 million each—and all of them end up plugged with cement. Twenty miles of drilling, straight down, 12 silent holes sleeping in the sea like small abandoned mine shafts, each of them only 6 inches in diameter at the bottom, each covering only a few square inches of the ocean's floor.

◆ ◆ ◆

Tourists in KL don't know about the oil. They do what tourists everywhere like to do: go sightseeing, go shopping, go dining and, eventually, go on to the airport. Perhaps the Ministry of Tourism survey was correct; for some there isn't enough to do. There is a "Chinatown" district to visit, several passable restaurants serving Indian and Chinese specialties, a national museum, the inevitable supper club revolving at the top of one of the big hotels and excursions into the nearby countryside to see pewter factories, tin mines, rubber plantations, a big limestone cave and "quaint Malay villages"—meaning a few tin-roof huts standing on stilts in the coconut and banana groves.

But if the packaged touring is predictable, there is also much natural beauty that is eye opening. In early summer, flame trees make scarlet splashes against the deep jungle greens and carpets of water hyacinths, blue as morning glories, spread in the milky waters of old abandoned mines. Towering above all are the awesome cumulous clouds that seem to go with the country, volcanoes of white and gray vapor born of jungle humidity and equatorial sun, an ever-changing mountain range that is a part of the landscape itself.

◆ ◆ ◆

Big John can make his own sort of volcano when he flows the well, but he doesn't want any accidental eruptions. His big torch sticks out over *North Star*'s side, a rectangular pipe 30 feet long with a blower at one end to force a draft and a collar of spraying water around the muzzle end. From two miles below, in the fetid, 350-degree darkness of the well, gas builds pressure. A system of pipes and valves diverts it to the burner.

"Watch out now!" said Big John. "Here she comes!" As he spoke, a cloud of black smoke with intestines of orange flame belched from the burner. The cooling water spray turned to steam, the flame burned bluer and brighter, roaring defiantly at the sea for a minute and a half. Then it went out. That was flowing the well.

Someone said, let's get a drink and we headed inside again.

Four meals a day are served on *North Star;* the kitchen and dining room never close. For an eating man, it's good duty. But having a drink doesn't mean beer or gin and tonic—it means orangeade, milk, or coffee. No alcohol allowed on the rig. And no women.

"Try the chocolate cake," said the chef. "Just fresh."

As the afternoon grew long, the chopper pilot was anxious to head for land again. We said our goodbyes, then lifted off and watched *North Star* diminish into a spot on the sea. It was dusk when we clattered down near the beach at Kuala Trengannu. A small twin-engine Navajo was waiting to take us on across the jungle and back to KL.

"No sweat," said the Navajo pilot, "good weather and the flight plan is filed. Let's go." Like Cal the tool pusher, Sam the pilot was a contractor to the oil company. I wondered if he'd flown with Chennault. He looked like the Flying Tiger type and he was old enough too.

We studied charts as we flew. Malaysia is a long, thin peninsula, reaching from Thailand in the north to Singapore at the south end. It is about 70 percent covered with one of the most inpenetrable of rain forests. Within this jungle live some of the world's most primitive people—pygmies, aborigines, headhunters—and, along the east coast, there are tigers. I switched off the map light and looked down at the dark plush carpet which softened the contours of the mountains it covered. At three thousand feet, the reality of what was below seemed remote; jungles are always green on maps, I thought. This one looks like all the others. But, of course, anyone who flies, even old pilots, always looks to earth with the unspoken question, "Could I get down if I had to?"

In a small plane over the Malay jungle, the answer is no. But the engines sounded healthy minute after minute and what could possibly lie ahead other than that Peking Duck dinner we'd been promising ourselves?

After the light of day and the gold of sunset was gone from our upper sky, the plane seemed to close in around us, as if it had lost wings and engines and all external parts and now consisted of a small cabin flying through darkness. The red glow from the instrument panel reflected on our four faces. Nobody talked. It was a perfect time to sleep after a long day on the sea, but the radio kept squawking, a party line full of chatter, orders and acknowledgements that I couldn't decipher. I did understand, however, that our Navajo had its own identification number which the pilot always used when he talked with the voice on the radio.

"We're going to have to go up," he said after a time. "Weather ahead." I couldn't see anything ahead, but thoughts of a martini somehow replaced my appetite for duck. I looked out the window at the steady green light on our wingtip. It seemed far away, almost detached from the plane. In the distance, beyond the light, another bigger light flickered in the sky and then went out.

"Storm," the pilot said, nodding toward the distant flashes. As he spoke, a great sheet of lightning illuminated a range of snow-covered alps. Their tops were much higher in the sky than we were. *Not alps, thunderheads,* I thought. I remembered that they could go up to 40,000 feet.

"How high can we fly?" I asked.

"No problem," the pilot said, sensing my concern. "We fly around that stuff. Or between."

Now we were talking to the tower at KL. Not yet, they were saying. We've got a couple of commercials in the area, diverted from Singapore by the storm. Stay where you are Navajo, they said. We'll clear you in shortly. The pilot talked about fuel and minutes.

Sometimes the lightning seemed to come from within the great towers of vapor, like a sputtering gaslight inside a paper lantern. Other flashes were as naked as swords. They lighted our faces.

English was now being spoken with an Italian accent on the radio. Alitalia 441 was holding. So was Swissair. There was talk about the weather in Bangkok. Our little plane pitched and bucked like a kite caught in summer gusts. We were in a valley now, towering cloud peaks on either side, their shapes etched hard on my eyes every time the white fire of the storm caught them. The engines wailed.

Alitalia sounded excited. I thought of where he was from, how I wouldn't mind having dinner in Piazza Navona tonight as long as there was this problem with KL. Swissair came in calm. *Accustomed to mountains,* I thought. Pilot Sam relaxed in his seat, a man who had seen all this before.

"Always this way in May and June," he said, his hands lightly on the controls. "You in a hurry?" he asked.

I said I wasn't. We talked about other things for a while. Sam said he never saw so many Japanese as there were in Malaysia now. "They're smart. They can show this country how to do a lot of things." I wasn't really listening.

After a few more minutes of bumping around the sky, the tower called our number. Sam shifted in his seat like a bus driver getting ready to leave the garage. "KL here we come," he said with patient good humor. Then he turned around to look at me.

"You didn't really want to see the agricultural regions of Malaysia tonight, did you?"

I said I would be happy to see the airport—like any other tourist.

CHAPTER II
Rain I Remember

RAIN IS NOT only the universal dread of travelers, it seems, but we're also somewhat ashamed if it falls on us. When we come home from a trip, one of the first reports we want to make to our friends is: "Had a wonderful time, no rain at all." Lack of precipitation becomes the measure of our success as vacationers. If it happens to rain at a place where the hotel rates are confidently based on a high percentage of sunshine, we'll suffer gray clouds for only a day or so, then pack up and leave, like selling a disappointing stock before the bottom drops out.

Travel guides, magazines and government brochures not only advise tourists on what to wear when visiting the temples at Kora Tobuku in August, but they often provide records on the average rainfall—the odds, as it were, on sunshine. Nothing guaranteed, you understand, but could the government tourist office be wrong?

Rain, alas, is seen as a defeat, a washout, a rotten break for anyone who gets but one well-deserved vacation a year—"and it should rain just then."

I remember the feeling of being cheated by rain. When I was a camper on Lake Sebago in Maine, a rainy day was a loss of that much of summer; it meant no baseball, swimming or sailing, just a morning spent in the woodworking shop making a magazine rack, all the while looking out the window for a brightening of the sky. Rain is not for kids.

But later, much later, my senses learned that rain has a rhythm that sunshine does not possess, that it can carry a scent from afar, make an indoor fire cozy, turn a plain landscape into something beautiful and mysterious or even force me to pay attention to a place I might not have noticed otherwise. I'm not saying that rain is fun, but it has often left me with memories that mere sunshine would never have created.

In Saltillo, on that August night long ago, we lingered in the small hotel bar, drinking rum cokes to pass the time. We said we were waiting for a Mexican cloudburst to end, but that wasn't true. We really didn't care whether the rain stopped or not because this was our honeymoon and there was a secret delight in being marooned by the storm.

That's part of it: rain demands a sort of philosophical surrender, an acknowledgement, a willingness to absorb rather than a frenzy to shed. What if that place you've waited all your life to see (and which has always appeared in golden sunshine in all the travel photos) is cloaked in gloom when it is your day at last? "Cloaked in gloom?" Well, if you insist, but perhaps there is another way to look at it. Gray can be a very interesting color, I have learned.

At Nikko National Park, 90 miles north of Tokyo, the temples are among the most ornate and colorful in Japan and the countryside is famed for its sweeping panoramas, plunging waterfalls and autumn foliage almost as brilliant as Vermont's. It is a spectacle to be seen on a lovely day if possible, of course, but October is fickle and cold rains and liquid fogs can settle on the mountains. When they do, they paint a new picture at Nikko.

On the day I remember, Japanese visitors of all ages and types were there despite the weather, many of the older women dressed in rich kimonos, holding British-looking umbrellas aloft as they walked uphill toward the shrines, a moving, bobbing procession of black hemispheres seen against the pale milk of fog. Overhead was the granite *torii,* a colossal arch giving no shelter, a twist of heavy hawser stretched between its uprights, water dripping from the rope to the flagstones below. Now and then the faint bluish blink of a tourist's camera flash made wet things shine briefly. The hollow sound of many wooden clogs hurried on ahead.

Nikko's temples are surrounded by a lofty forest of ancient cedar trees. Their trunks, cinnamon brown in sunlight, were sodden black shafts now, thrusting up into the fog, holding up the sky like the columns of a cathedral.

On a fine day, Nikko's vermillion pagoda has five stories and reaches 115 feet to the treetops. In the rain, with its head lost in swirling vapor, the pagoda was not shorter, however, but taller than ever, a giant of infinite height now, a many-tiered ladder to heaven with only its lower rungs visible. Five stories? Or five hundred? I could only imagine.

Some day I shall see Nikko again, no doubt, and the sun may shine and the brilliance of the lacquers and the gleam of the gold will dazzle my eyes with the pleasure of color. All the same, I know I will always remember the Nikko I saw in the rain, full of misty moods, its black outlines as finely drawn as a calligrapher's purest strokes.

Sometimes rain is businesslike, arriving each day when it is expected, like a visitor who has a frequent appointment. In those regions of the world where it rains every afternoon there is a reassurance about the event. The streets are washed and the cisterns replenished and the palms and bamboo are given a good shower to refresh their greenness. No one looks up in surprise when an afternoon rain hits Singapore. Life is arranged accordingly and even tourists don't begrudge an hour or so under cover at Raffle's Bar as long as they are assured that "this always happens."

I stopped at Majuro in the Marshall Islands once, just looking for a couple of quiet days in the sun. It is an unlikely place to go for recreation, a thin crescent of an island with a big new airstrip and a pathetic main street several miles long. I assumed it might be a place to stretch out on a beach, however; Karen and I had endured some long days of monsoon rains in other parts of the Pacific and we felt like drying out.

The Gateway Motel is a two-story, all-plywood wonder which throbs like a log drum when guests walk along its open-air corridors. The owner-manager, an easy going island type in a sport shirt and a big hat, picks you up at the edge of the airstrip in a yellow truck. He knows right away that you are probably his responsibility when you get off the plane. There is one other hotel on the island, but the Gateway gets all the important trade, meaning the people with baggage, wearing shoes and not chewing betel nut.

Adjacent to the motel, facing the lagoon, the Gateway operates a thatched-roof annex which is a combined beach house, bar and dining room. Several hungry but amiable mongrel dogs make this their home. They hang around the small kitchen when meals are being prepared, then join the guests at the tables when the food is served.

At night, colored lights hang under the thatch and the hot pink glare of a juke box gives the place the look of a jungle nightclub. A husky, off-duty cop acts as bouncer and enforcer of the local law that everyone must have a drinking license, obtainable for $1 from the police.

There was a glorious sunset the evening we arrived, made more spectacular by a sky full of clouds. The clouds contained rain. When it was night, we sat under the thatch of the annex, drinking beer and listening to an invisible torrent falling through the darkness all around.

We joined some other Americans at a table near the edge of the darkness. Water poured from the bottom of the thatch like a curtain of glass beads caught in the light. Our group of fellow travelers consisted of an inspector for the Federal Aviation Agency who was on a periodic swing around the islands, a representative of the large construction firm which had built the new airstrip and two Air Force doctors from Hawaii who were on temporary duty and attending to some public health problems on the island.

We all began talking in a rush of conviviality, like five people in a lifeboat, no one knowing how long it would be until rescue. Then the beer and the greasy food quieted us. The dogs slept and the beer cans left pools of sweat on the table. The rain was so loud it made conversation difficult anyway.

The next day, the rain continued. It was a visible force now, peening the surface of the lagoon with its billions of tiny, meteoric landings, beating the blue water to gray. It seemed worse because we knew there wouldn't be another flight out of Majuro for 48 hours. The hotel manager said, yes, it might rain that long, it often did.

I remembered seeing bad movies in which artificial rain had obviously been made with fire hoses, letting clumsy splashes of water fall on the actors. The rain at Majuro was like that. It hit the ground and bounced.

By the third day, we were stir crazy. We had by now given names to all the dogs, solicited as much free medical advice as was decent from the two doctors, learned all about the potential hazards of night landings from the FAA man and developed an intense dislike for the contractor's rep. Between downpours, we walked along an old abandoned World War II airstrip, now littered with weeds and beer cans. One of the motel dogs came with us and we were glad for his company.

When it was time to go, we got ourselves down to the airport almost two hours before our plane was due to arrive and we cheered when we saw it grow from a speck in the sky into a beautiful Boeing that would carry us away. We hadn't had a minute on a beach, we were bored to anger—but we had learned something about ourselves that would be a yardstick for the future: how much we could take. From this time on we could always say, "It's not as bad as Majuro" and feel better right away.

If it hadn't rained, all we would have experienced was a couple of easily forgotten days in the sun.

CHAPTER 12
The Meat No Money Can Buy

JAPAN IS A COUNTRY of myths and legends, many of them beyond a Westerner's capacity to comprehend or even to believe. There is, for example, the strange story of Japanese beef —the so-called Kobe variety—and how it is produced.

"The cattle are fed nothing but beer . . . they are kept constantly in the dark . . . small children massage the cow's muscles every day . . . they are never permitted to have sex . . . they are fed wild rice . . . they get a shot of sake for breakfast . . . they are washed once a week in a solution of green tea . . . they are given raw fish as a tonic . . . they are never allowed out in a pasture . . . they are slaughtered by Shinto priests . . . they are made drunk before they are killed so their muscles will relax in death."

I had heard such stories for years. The first man who told me was a young Japanese army officer who had survived four years of near starvation on Wake Island and who couldn't stop talking about food. The second was a student from the hotel management school at Cornell who was working as a steward on a

New York Central Railroad dining car. The third was a New York public relations man who could fold paper, Japanese fashion, into the shape of 25 animals.

I did not regard any of these as particularly reliable sources of information, yet the legend of Japan's happy, delicious cows fascinated me. At last, I decided the next time I was in Japan I would really try to get to the bottom of the mystery. Was it fact or just a good story?

In Tokyo, I knew some people who, by profession, might be expected to have some answers. One was Kinjiro Ikezawa, then executive manager of the New Otani hotel. There are 11 restaurants in this big, first-class establishment and they serve a lot of beef.

Ikezawa suggested that the most sociable way to both sample and discuss the subject would be at dinner at his top restaurant, the Kioi. We slipped out of our shoes and shuffled along the tatami mats to a private dining room and settled down, cross-legged, to analyze an almost theatrical meal of *sukiyaki, teriyaki* and other beef specialties. My host had ordered the best, of course, so chewing was no problem. A toothless infant could have eaten everything we were served. Our elegantly dressed, middle aged waitress who announced her comings and going with only the rustle of kimono silks, kept our bowls filled with helpings from a simmering pot between us.

"Do you believe those old stories about feeding beer to the cows?" I asked the veteran hotelman. "Or are they just another Japanese legend?"

"Well, I have heard those stories, just as you have," Ikezawa said, "but I don't know how much truth there is to them. One thing I can tell you, though. I would be glad to use American beef or Australian beef in our restaurants because they are cheaper than our own Japanese beef. Unfortunately, they are just not good enough to satisfy any top Japanese chef."

U.S. beef not good enough!

"If that surprises you," Ikezawa said, "why don't you talk to our head butcher? Perhaps he will explain."

Hiroshi Nakamoto, a young man all in white, buys $6000 worth of beef for his hotel every day. He also supervises the cutting of 900 pounds of beef carcass for the special needs of Japanese dishes. His "office" is a big white-tiled, steam-cleaned butcher room in the hotel basement where he works with a staff of assistants and apprentices.

"How expensive is Kobe beef these days?" I asked, for openers.

"About $7 a pound," he said, giving me the exact price in yen and kilos. Younger butchers were chopping and carving the precious red meat at huge cutting tables. Nakamoto kept his stern eye on them as we talked, occasionally directing a certain tray of cuts to a refrigerator or a special storage rack.

I asked him if Kobe beef was the only type he would use for the hotel menus.

"Actually," he explained, almost all Japanese prime beef *is* Kobe. That's where it comes from, the region around Kobe." Kobe is a seaport city almost 400 miles southwest of Tokyo on the Inland Sea. It is in Kansai Province—"and Kansai is to Japanese beef what Kansas is to your wheat," Nakamoto added, seemingly proud that he could display this much knowledge of the U.S.

"But we also have good beef in my country," I said. "Have you ever used American beef?" Nakamoto nodded his head, yes, his chef's hat wagging, but his face was without expression. "It's good meat, isn't it?" I prompted.

"U.S. beef is good for barbecues," Nakamoto said, garbling the word somewhat, but still obviously pleased that he could say it at all. "No barbecues in Japan," he added politely.

"What about those stories of how the Kobe beef is raised?" I asked. "Have you ever seen cows getting a rubdown in their stalls?"

"No, I have not seen," Nakamoto admitted, "but everyone has heard those stories. I think it happened in old Japan. Not today."

Not today. Probably not, I conceded to myself. Who could afford to raise beef that way. It was foolish to think that this was anything but the ghost of an old legend that I was pursuing. All the same, I had now discovered that Japanese beef was (1) delicious, (2) expensive, and (3) preferred over the U.S. variety. There had to be reasons for all this. I decided to keep looking and asking.

Noriko Shishiuchi is a pretty young Japanese public relations girl on the staff of the Tokyo Hilton. She invited me to enlarge my knowledge of Japanese beef by trying a specialty called *ishiyaki* at the hotel's handsome Genji restaurant.

Superheated rocks the size of pumpernickel loaves were brought directly to our table from seven hours in an electric oven. First our waitress lubricated the stones by rubbing them with a chunk of beef fat firmly pinched between chopsticks. Then thin strips of beef were laid on the stones to grill along with a delicate assortment of fresh vegetable slices. The stones were so hot and the food so expertly sliced that cooking time per morsel was only a minute or less. As before, I found the meat amazingly tender.

"What do you know about the Kansai 'cattle country'?" I asked Noriko.

"It's not really cattle country the way you think," she said with a pretty smile. "You must remember that the eating of meat in Japan began only a century ago and it has only become a big business very recently. Before the Meiji period, it was against most people's religion to eat meat at all."

And had she heard those stories about Kobe beef?

"Yes, of course," Noriko said, "but it's not just around Kobe. If I were you, I should look in some out of the way places to find cattle being raised in exotic ways."

"But where?"

"I'm not sure," she said apologetically. "Omi, perhaps . . ."

If I was not getting far in my quest for facts, I was certainly developing an appreciation for Japanese beef in the process.

In New York, the Benihana restaurants are popular even with people who may know little about Japanese cuisine but who like good beef and appreciate a little showmanship with their dining. "When you get to Tokyo, you should talk to our head chef about Kobe beef," owner Rocky Aoki had said.

Nobutsugu Fujisaku is a big, jolly man who has been cooking and teaching others to cook for nearly a half century. He heads the Benihana school for chefs—the place where young Japanese are taught the intricate knife-play that amuses Benihana guests everywhere. Fujisaku carries his own carving knife in a scabbard at his belt. He was all ready for me in his sparkling chef's uniform when I came to lunch.

"For you, I will prepare everything myself," he said, indicating several dishes of sliced beef ready and waiting. "Today I give two demonstrations, one for you, the American journalist, and then again on television this afternoon." Fujisaku, I had been told, is much in demand as an expert on Japanese cooking. He prepared a multi-course treat for me, a combination of *teppanyaki* preparations, all cut, trimmed, minced, sliced, seasoned, cooked and served right under my nose. Although we talked, Fujisaku's hands never stopped until the last piece of beef had been sprinkled with sesame seeds and put on my dish.

"Good water and good rice make good beef," the master chef said. "That is what make's Kobe beef so good. We pay at least $6 a pound, but the price can be even double that for fancier grades. The trouble is, the term 'Kobe' has become so famous that many restaurants say they're serving it when they are not."

And the stories about beer and massage and exotic diets?

"I believe them," he said. "I'm sure there are still some places where this is done. Not right around Kobe, perhaps, but somewhere . . ."

Somewhere, somewhere. Was there still a chance?

Before I left New York, Mike Shinohara of Japan Air Lines had said, "If it's beef you're interested in, be sure to try *shabu-shabu*. I'll have Tad Fujimatsu arrange it for you. You may find that he can also answer some of your questions about Kobe."

At the Zakuro restaurant, in Tokyo's Akasaka district, just across from the American Embassy, *shabu-shabu* is a production. Zakuro is famous with Americans and Japanese alike for the quality of the beef it serves. JAL's Fujimatsu and I were ushered into a small private room where we slipped out of our shoes and slid across the tatami to a low table with a pit beneath it. The pit is called a *kodatsu* and it provides westerners with a comfortable way of sitting without folding the legs into yoga positions.

A large copper urn was brought and placed at the center of the table. The urn was half filled with water, then a metal cylinder like a stove pipe, sealed at the bottom, was immersed into the center of the urn and filled with hot coals. Soon the water in the urn came to a hissing boil. It is this sound, like a freshly poured glass of ginger ale, which gives *shabu-shabu* its name.

Next, a large platter arrived spread with the now familiar

slices of beautifully marbled beef. When lifted deftly between chopsticks, light passed through the thin flesh like a flame through parchment.

Fujimatsu told me what to do. "Pick up a piece of meat with the chopsticks, dip it quickly into the boiling water—not too long!—then take it out and dip it into this sauce." The sauce is called *gomadare* and it is made from sesame seeds, among other things.

The meat was so clear and tender that even boiling it did not toughen it or hurt the flavor. It only turned the color from rare red to cooked brown.

"You can only do this with Kobe beef," Fujimatsu said. Later, after the water had been turned into a thin broth from much dipping of the meat, fresh vegetables and bean curd were added for a second course. Finally, the broth itself is served.

"Is all Japanese beef this good?" I asked, "or am I making the mistake of letting you impress me with luxury?"

"It's true," said Fujimatsu, "not all of our meat is as good as Kobe. There is some beef raised around Tokyo, for example, but it is considered inferior. Kobe is the best commercial grade, no question. This is because it comes only from a certain kind of cattle called Tajima. But I think what you really want to know about is not really Kobe beef, but *Matsusaka beef.* That is the *very* best; too rare ever to be commercial."

Suddenly, two new names: Tajima and Matsusaka. Where had they been? Where would they lead me?

"I'd like you to visit our flight kitchens," Fujimatsu said. "If we go out tomorrow, you could meet a rather remarkable man. He is Mizuguchi, JAL's head chef. If anybody can tell you what you want to know about these beef legends, he's the one."

Takio Mizuguchi is a small man, even by Japanese standards. With his tall white chef's hat on, he looks about 5–6, not more.

In his mid-fifties, he has been cooking all his life he says. He has been with JAL since 1960 and now presides not only as head chef but as managing director of the airline's huge kitchen facilities. This giant food factory turns out vast quantities of everything from artistic pastries to tender filets on a 24-hour-a-day, 7-day-a-week schedule. In a single year, his kitchens prepare 130 *tons* of beef for use on JAL flights and the flights of more than 20 other major airlines which contract with JAL for food service out of Tokyo.

When Mizuguchi puts on his tall white hat and steps into the kitchens, it is like a commanding general on a white-glove inspection. He took me first to the meat cutting room and ordered some trays of freshly cut filets brought from the refrigerator.

"We use nothing but Kobe," he said, "with the exception of about 8000 pounds a year of U.S. prime rib loins which I think are better than Japanese beef for roasting."

The tray of filets was uniformly perfect, each 2-inch-thick cut carefully wrapped with a thin circlet of white fat tied on with two turns of butcher twine. Mizuguchi looked at them approvingly. I asked how much meat like this cost.

"Because we buy in such large quantities, we pay just under $5 per pound. We could buy Australian beef for less, but it is not as good. U.S. beef is better than Australian and very uniform in quality—but, of course, there is only one Kobe beef in the world."

I asked about the legends—the tipsy cows led to slaughter.

"You are talking about what I call the *champagne* of beef— the cattle raised on small farms in the Matsusaka region. I have seen these many years ago. Sometimes they have as many as 40 or 50 head of cattle, but usually less. The meat is superb. It is like Kobe beef but made even better by special feeding. It costs about $12 a pound when you can get it."

"There is one farm called Wadakin, I think," Mizuguchi said. "They are quite well known in the region. They raise their own cattle and still do all the traditional things . . ."

The trail was getting hot!

Matsusaka is a medium-size Japanese city about 250 miles from Tokyo in Kansai. It has an ordinary railway station where you carry your own bags and hope to find someone who can speak English. Fortunately, my cab driver seemed to understand when I said "Wadakin."

Within five minutes we stopped in front of a prosperous looking restaurant on the main street. The building was natural wood, aged dark brown in color and the entryway was a spacious area cobbled with smooth stones. I stopped here to put my shoes with dozens of pairs already deposited by other luncheon guests. An attendant looked at my collection of camera gear and around-the-world baggage as if it were a curious and excessive load for a gentleman to be bringing to lunch. Nevertheless, he indicated he would take charge of everything and showed me the way to enter.

Matsusaka may be Japanese boondocks, but the Wadakin is no hick establishment. There are many dining rooms, large, small and private on three floors and the decor is first class. I was asked to wait in a private dining room until someone who could speak English would help me. Americans traveling alone are pretty conspicuous anywhere outside the tourist regions of Japan.

The young woman who soon arrived was Yuko Matsuda. She explained that she was the owner's daughter. I said I had come to find out more about the famous Matsusaka beef. Miss Matsuda seemed to understand and said that her father would be very flattered and would join us later. In the meantime, she proposed a special lunch consisting of Wadakin beef prepared in a variety of ways.

The moment had arrived. The Pilgrim was in Mecca. Good as Japanese beef had seemed up to now, I was sure I was about to enjoy the ultimate. I sat, feeling almost reverential, crossed my legs tailor fashion and waited for the curtain to go up on the first act.

A kimono-clad hostess shuffled silently into the room, dropped gracefully to her knees and placed a copper brazier filled with fiery charcoal in the center of the round table.

We began with *amiyaki*—small steaks of about a quarter pound each, brushed lightly with a special sauce, grilled on a wire mesh over the glowing charcoal. The hostess explained that *amiyaki* steaks are so choice that only about 10 pounds of such meat is obtained from each 1500 pound beef animal when it is butchered.

The *amiyaki* was juicy with its own marble-pattern fat, faintly seasoned, a meat delicacy to rival anything I had ever eaten. The *sukiyaki* which followed, although a more familiar dish to an American, was better than I had ever known. The thin slices of beef seemed to cook in a half minute or less when dropped into the iron pot full of bubbling broth and fresh vegetables.

Takeyasu Matsuda is the third generation proprietor of Wadakin. His grandfather, Kinbei Matsuda founded this particular dynasty of beef in 1870. He was followed in the company by his son, Shigero Matsuda, now retired.

After lunch, Matsuda and his daughter took me on a tour of the business. We went first across the street to a butcher shop where all the beef is dressed, then on to a barn where some of the prize cattle are kept for special fattening before slaughter. Along the way, Matsuda told me the long-sought story of the world's most exotic beef and how it got that way.

Until the beginning of the Meiji period in Japan, he explained, very few Japanese ate meat of any kind, but when customs changed, the founding Matsuda, a farmer in Matsusaka, bought a few young cows from dairymen and began to fatten them according to some theories of his own—high protein mash and beer.

"What does beer do for the meat?" I asked as we walked through a big barn where black cows, each in an individual stall, watched us from their stanchions.

"Beer is nourishing, of course," said Matsuda, "but it has always been our belief that a quart a day helps give the animals a better appetite. When we do not give beer, our cows do not eat as much." Wadakin farms use standard brands of Japanese beer.

The Matsudas raise only the shortlegged Tajimas which come from Kobe, 200 miles to the north. They buy 8-month old calves at auction—"virgin females only," is the way Matsuda describes them. Two years later, these animals weigh 1300 to 1400 pounds and are ready for slaughter. As for the story that they die blissfully intoxicated, Matsuda says it is not true. They are killed in a local slaughter house and, albeit sober, they suffer no death trauma.

Although the Matsudas claim to have started the highly specialized Matsusaka beef business a century ago, they are not the only company raising cattle there now. The region and its methods have achieved such a reputation that demand always exceeds the supply of beef, even at those prices.

Nowadays, Wadakin can not buy enough calves in the open market to supply its needs, so Matsuda has been forced to start breeding his own stock again, something that his grandfather gave up. He has over 1000 head of Tajimas on a nearby farm. They are allowed limited grazing in small pastures until they are two years old. At this time they are brought to the fattening barn where from 40 to 60 animals are kept on the glutonous diet that adds 250 pounds to their weight in only 6 months.

I watched a mash being prepared. A woman worker measured ingredients into big wooden tubs: rice hay, finely chopped and made tender by steaming; Australian barley; bran; soy bean meal, pressed to remove the oils; salt; dry cracked corn; mineral oils; vitamin B; calcium; fish meal flour. The surly looking black animals stuck their muzzles into the food and made snorting sounds of pleasure as they ate. Every meal is a feast.

"Now tell me about the massage," I asked. "Is that true?"

"This is an essential part of the program," Matsuda explained. "The massage takes 15 minutes for each cow each day and it helps to distribute the animal's fat throughout the meat instead of allowing it to build up in a layer under the skin."

Matsuda ordered a stablehand to take one of the cows from a stall and demonstrate the massage for me. The animal was led outside and tethered to a post. The handler picked up a quart bottle of water-clear rice wine, filled his mouth with it until his cheeks bulged, then in one explosive burst, sprayed the *sake* all over the cow's flanks. Up and down both sides of the animal the man went, filling his mouth and spewing forth the liquor in great clouds of spray until the animal's coat was wet and shiny. He then grabbed a tight bundle of rice straw about 10 inches long and 2 inches thick and proceeded to rub the alcohol into the cow's hide in a vigorous massage that lasted at least 10 minutes.

I was astounded—even though I had only witnessed one part of the oft-told legend. "What in the world does the *sake* do for the cow?" I asked.

Matsuda shrugged a little as if it were a matter that was really out of his hands.

"We have always done it," he said. "In the old days, the

alcohol was considered an antiseptic, a cure against diseases. Now we use chemicals for this, but we still use the *sake* as a part of the daily massage."

I asked if the handler ever took a swallow of the *sake* himself during the spraying operation. Everyone laughed at the question, but no one answered it.

"Can you show me how a cow drinks beer too?" I asked.

Matsuda gave another order and, as quickly as he had produced the quart of sake, the handler produced a quart of Kirin beer. It was the same brand I had just enjoyed with my lunch. Grasping the cow by a ring through its nose, the man shoved the neck of the bottle into the animal's mouth. As soon as the suds began to flow, the cow sucked on the bottle like a baby, spilling hardly a drop until the quart was drained.

Now I had seen it all. Whether the *sake* shampoo and beer appetizer were merely a contemporary reenactment of a genuine historical tradition, I could not be sure, but I had seen it. It happens.

I asked Matsuda where all his beef was sold. He said a good deal of the farm's production was used in their own restaurant, some went to a small retail butcher shop in town where local people could buy what they could afford. "But the prime cuts are reserved for our special customers in Tokyo, like the New Otani hotel and some others, the Yugiri restaurant in the Ginza and Zakuro" (where I had had *shabu-shabu*).

I told Matsuda that the *amiyaki* I had had for lunch was magnificent. "How much does that cut of meat cost per pound?" I asked, remembering that only 10 pounds came from every carcass.

"You liked our *amiyaki?*" Matsuda smiled knowingly. "Most people do. But we never sell that. We keep it to serve only at the Wadakin. No money could buy it . . ."

CHAPTER 13
On the Border of Terror

WHEN SPRING comes to Israel's rugged Naftali Mountains, fresh blooming poppies are as brilliant on the Lebanese side of the border as they are to the south. On a clear day, a visitor can stand on high ground and see the brooding Golan Heights to the east and the lush Huleh Valley below. A few goats graze along the rocky hillsides and a pair of 8-power binoculars will pick out an occasional Arab shepherd north of the border.

The binoculars belong to Captain Benny Nativ, one of the Israeli border police force. "Look up there," he says, pointing toward a barren mountain ridge just across the line in Lebanon. "See what seems to be a stone wall, but the stones are not the same color as the ones around them? That is one of their observation points. They are in there now, probably watching us, just as we are watching them."

Nativ means the enemy—Palestinian guerillas. Using Lebanon as a base of operations against Israel, the terrorists have turned this border area into a place of fear and death. It comes in many forms, always suddenly and without pattern or warn-ing.

"It looks peaceful now, doesn't it?" says Nativ, "but in two minutes, right where we stand, it could be all upside down."

"Upside down" can mean several things—sniping small arms fire on the border police jeep, or a single mortar shell lobbing into an Israeli village. It can mean bazooka fire, TNT charges, land mines, 130mm Katyusha rocket fire launched in salvos against settlements. As the world now knows, it can also mean infiltration by terrorists headed for such Israeli towns as Qiryat Shemona and Maalot.

There may be no defense against rocket fire, but there is some against infiltration. The first line of that defense is Captain Nativ and the force under his command at Metzudat (fortress) Yesha. Built by the British about 35 years ago, the fort stands on high ground two kilometers south of the border. From the valley below it looks like a square blockhouse with a tall obser-vation tower. It is reached after a grinding, 2000-foot low-gear climb by jeep.

Although the time and the terrain are all wrong and the men of the post wear the rough khaki of the Israeli army or the green beret of the border police, there is a feeling of French Foreign Legion about the old fort. It is a 3-story stone and cement structure built four square around an inner courtyard. A heavy steel door pockmarked with shellholes from earlier battles opens on the yard. The round tower is about 6 stories high with windows and firing slits. Barbed wire, gleaming and new, is stretched in concertina rolls around the outer perimeter of the area. A few small outbuildings, an armorer's magazine and a motor pool garage complete the layout. There are a number of jeeps, some larger Dodge Power Wagons with machinegun mounts and two brutish-looking armored personnel carriers parked near the fort.

Captain Nativ is a husky 210 pounds whose grip is strong and smile friendly. "Welcome to the border," he says as he comes out the steel doors. "You're interested in my armored cars, I see. They're called El Walid—Egyptian—captured in the Six Day War. No damn good, either, but we need everything we can get. They have German engines, French tires and Egyptian design. If you stay on the paved road with them, they're all right, but if you get into mud, you will certainly be stuck."

Nativ's small office has a military map of the border area on the wall, another on his desk. Both are heavily marked to indicate patrol roads, lookout points, places where there has been rocket fire on towns, civilians kidnapped, reservoirs dynamited, power lines destroyed, irrigation systems damaged, soldiers killed.

"You see this?" says Nativ, holding a piece of something that looks like an aluminum pipe about 5 inches in diameter. Both ends are shredded and torn by explosive force. "We picked it up in the village of Dishon near here. It is Katyusha, the 130mm Russian-made rocket. It had hit a house and destroyed it. By a miracle, no one was inside.

"And see this—more Russian." Nativ held up a khaki colored cannister, about 3 feet long, which had held a bazooka shell. "I use it for a map case now."

Israelis have become as skilled at using their enemies' captured arms as the Viet Cong once were. "Why not?" Nativ asks. "They have good stuff. The Kalachnikov automatic assault rifle is none better. It is light, simple, rugged. It is what I carry myself!" He slips the weapon off his shoulder, drops the curved clip of bullets out, clears the chamber with a harsh clang and hands the gun to his visitor. "Feel it," he says. A lieutenant in the room swings his Kalachnikov off his shoulder too and agrees. It is a good gun.

"You want to see the border, come on," says Nativ, plugging the ammo clip back into the gun. In the courtyard he leaves orders, speaking fast in Hebrew. Then he signals one enlisted man to come along for extra firepower and swings behind the wheel of his jeep.

The road toward the border is macadam and is still used by normal traffic although cars are few. Nativ talks as he drives. He is full of enthusiasm for his work, full of conviction that his sector of his country's frontier must be protected at all costs. Every few minutes he picks up the radio-telephone handset from under the jeep dashboard to communicate with the fort or with other vehicles out on patrol. His eyes roam the surrounding hillsides constantly as he drives.

"They are not so brave, these Fatah, you know," he says. "They will not attack me. They only want to kill our civilians. It doesn't take a very brave man to put a bomb under a schoolhouse full of children. That is murder. And they won't even do it without using a timing device so they have time to get away themselves. Three sticks of Czechoslovak TNT and a Chinese alarm clock and then, in a little while, boom!"

Nativ's jeep passes through young orchards where peach and plum trees are just reaching crop-bearing age. Younger pecan trees looking like small, straight sticks are planted by the thousands in long straight rows. "Our people are making something out of this land. This is not occupied Arab territory. It has been ours since the foundation of the state," Nativ says. "It will take more than dynamite to scare us away."

Palestinian infiltrators move across the border at night—to terrorize local Israeli farmers and kibbutz members with random terror. They also plant mines in the roads patrolled by Nativ's men.

"If we see them at night," says Nativ, "we shoot only to kill. We have taken no prisoners. We know we are killing the right ones because they usually wear camouflage suits, distinctive rubber-soled shoes made in Czechoslovakia—and they carry the Kalachnikov."

The jeep climbed higher now along a narrow road. "See the two trees ahead?" Nativ asks. "The one on the right is in Lebanon." It is difficult, if not impossible, to see this border without a guide. A few old tin signs with faded lettering mark the actual line. The jeep stops and Nativ and the enlisted man get out. The captain scans Lebanon with his binoculars.

"See over there? There are two Arabs sitting on some stones and another is walking along with the goats. It is a good sign. If there were Fatah in the area, you would see no one. There is something in the air when they are around." Nativ rubs the fingers of one hand together under his nose to suggest the smell of fear that the enemy puts on the wind.

"Sometimes they shoot at us in daylight. Only last week they wounded one of my men along this road. It is usually just one burst of machinegun fire and often at an impossible range, maybe 400 yards." Nativ shakes his head. "We call these crazy men—*kamikazi*—somebody who just wants to kill or be killed for Allah."

Now the jeep reaches a switchback in the mountain road. There is a spectacular view of the Huleh Valley below. It was here that Jews drained the proverbial swamps long before Israel was a nation. And it was here that Syrian guns once pounded the valley farmers with shellfire before the fall of Golan in the Six Day War. Now the valley seems at peace. Great rectangles of gleaming water mark the ponds where carp are raised for gefilte fish production. Other rectangles of green and brown represent the richest cotton land in Israel.

"Even though the Fatah have done nothing to frighten us away," says Nativ, "I must admit they are getting better. They are clever at infiltration. They have learned how much explosives to use to do a certain job. They camouflage their land mines better.

"But they could not operate as they do if they were not quartered and fed by the Lebanese. But I think the Lebanese should be frightened by now. They know we have suffered hundreds of atrocities at the hands of these murderers. They should also know that Israelis have a phrase which means in English, 'the account is full . . .' "

If Nativ has a grudging respect for the growing professionalism of his enemy, he has none for the Lebanese. "They could stop all this if they wanted to," he says. "Before Fatah came, we used to see Lebanese soldiers along this border and we knew them and sometimes we spoke with them. But where are they now that we need them? Gone!" Nativ swings his arms wide.

Again the jeep stops and Nativ backs slowly onto the shoulder of the road to turn around. "You see those tire tracks where I turn?" he asks. "That is my insurance. It is an old saying, 'When you cross a minefield, always step in someone else's footprints.' When I see tire tracks, I know there can be no mine under them."

Ahead there are signs of torn up macadam where a culvert passes under the road. "Two nights ago, Fatah came here with 15 pounds of explosive and blew this bridge. The border is just there—20 feet away. We put in a new culvert yesterday. Tomorrow we will probably replace the macadam. It may seem a senseless thing to do to destroy a little thing like this, but they want to keep us off the roads with fear."

On the way back to the fort, one of the El Walid vehicles approached on the road, stopped as Nativ waved from his jeep.

Five or six young Israelis man a machinegun and mortar in the rear. For the next two or three hours they will patrol. From high ground across the border, Fatah will no doubt watch them. Maybe one of the kamikazis will decide to shoot—and if his aim is good, the evening newscasts in Tel Aviv and Jerusalem will begin with the phrase which all Israelis have learned to dread.

"Today, on the Lebanese border, one of our soldiers was killed by Arab terrorists . . ."

CHAPTER 14

My Kind of Hotel

TWENTY-FIVE OR MORE years ago, I knew very little about hotels and had no idea that a time would come in my life when I would be familiar with hundreds of them around the world. In my youth, hotels were remote and expensive places in far cities, palaces for transients where one "put up" for the night when making a trip. If you were a kid living in a small town in Depression-doomed Massachusetts, an overnight stay at the Statler in Boston seemed an extravagant event and you concluded that something mighty important must be going on or you wouldn't be there. (I remember falling asleep on big pillows, listening to the music of the Cliquot Club Eskimos on the radio. Imagine, a radio *and* a bath with every room!)

Later in my boyhood, I remember the Regent Palace on Piccadilly where I fell asleep looking at the illuminated signs of that famous London crossroads, including my favorite, OXO bouillon, which blinked on and off like the tick-tock of time itself. Again, being in a hotel signified a landmark event in my life; in this case, my first trip out of the U.S. Hotels began to

138

seem like glamorous and exciting places, handmaidens to great events.

Magazines such as *Popular Mechanics* used to publish articles in those days which predicted that travelers would someday cross the Atlantic by air, hopping from one man-made seaplane base to the next and on each there would be a "hotel of the future," an island of safety and refuge in mid-ocean. Later in the Thirties, I also read about Pan American Airways' hotel at its Clipper base on Wake Island—and wasn't that just about the most remote place in the world? It seemed as strange and exciting an idea as a stateroom on the dirigible *Hindenburg* —which, after all, was a sort of hotel in the sky.

In a few more years, I came to think of hotels in a more sophisticated way. Even in Franklin, Mass., I'd heard that to rendezvous with a girl in a hotel, one had to have baggage— and *she* should be wearing a wedding ring or a reasonable facsimile because there were house detectives who checked on these details.

Thanks to movies such as *Weekend at the Waldorf,* hotels also acquired a certain theatrical image; they were places where Big Bands played in grand ballrooms which the announcer always described as being "high above" the city.

When war came, hotels were full of people in uniforms, meeting and parting. History was in the air—and in the lobby. When I was drafted, my co-workers at the tap and die factory gave me a going-away party at a hotel in Boston. We drank rye and ginger that night and I thought the girl I was with was beautiful and the comedian absolutely the greatest. Once more, I associated a hotel with an important event in my life. Such worldliness! In the men's room, cartoons of Hitler and Mussolini were painted on the urinals and you certainly didn't see anything like that in Franklin! I gave the attendant a big tip after he asked me if I needed rubbers.

The first hotel I fell in love with, truly in love with, was a beautiful pile of pink stucco enthroned at the very edge of the blue sea—the Royal Hawaiian on Waikiki Beach. It was my wartime dream. I thought it must be one of the most glamorous hotels in the world, and I remember the first time I walked under the towering *porte cochere* and stepped into the broad, airy lobby. There, at the other end, I could see straight onto the beach and the blue Pacific. There was no air conditioning, none was needed. Upstairs, every room had louvered doors and the tradewinds swept right down the halls. Servicemen could use the Royal's beach plus a locker, towel and shower without charge. The residents of the hotel were mostly Navy men, bearded submariners with gold earrings, back from long cruises under the sea, their white skin quickly turned red by the first few hours under the Waikiki sun.

I left Hawaii and the dream hotel and went on to the war zones where the only hotels were quonset huts which GIs had nicknamed Wotje Waldorf and Rongelap Ritz. (I wasn't the only one, apparently, who remembered hotels fondly.) Eventually, I also saw all that was left of Pan Am's brave hotel on Wake, a twisted skeleton of structural steel.

One day on Kwajalein I found a picture of the Royal Hawaiian in a magazine and it made me homesick. It had been almost a year since I'd seen Hawaii. I cut out the picture and pinned it to the wall next to Sherry Britton. I wanted to go back there in the worst way. Somehow I knew that if I ever saw the Royal again, it would be because the war was over.

I've returned to Waikiki a few times in the last 25 years. My old sweetheart, the Royal, is changed of course, but not too much. I still see the spot where the wartime beer garden was and I remember where the ping-pong tables were on the front lawn. It doesn't take much to bring back 1944.

Postwar, I began to make friends with other hotels in other ways. They were still the setting for important moments in my life. The Tiger in Columbia, Missouri, for example, where I arrived one night like a hick kid ready to enter the big university and fully expecting to be taken into a fraternity the next day. I ended up in a rooming house and washing dishes at the Tiger.

Then, later, there was the famous old Meuhlbach in Kansas City where, one memorable night, I became engaged during a fraternity party—soon followed by a honeymoon at the Gran Ancira in Monterrey, Mexico.

All of which, concerning my relations with hotels, is merely prologue in a way, a period of innocence and discovery. In the last two decades I have outgrown the notion that just being in a hotel signified a landmark event in my life. As a working journalist I began to check in and check out of so many Hiltons, Bellevues, Sheratons, Grands and Intercontinentals that it was like being caught in a revolving door with a too-big suitcase. The bell captains' uniforms no longer impressed me, nor the grand ballrooms, nor the celebrities in the lobby. What became more important than glamour was an ingredient I'd never looked for in younger years—the feeling that a hotel should be a home away from home, a place where a traveler's needs are not only well understood but also well "looked after," to use that homely old British expression.

Needless to say, I have discovered by now that not every hotel in the world provides tender, loving care, but a professional traveler accepts that reality and takes the good with the bad. It has made for a colorful collection of memories.

The Excelsior in Rome, for example, is an important address, full of Americans who make a loud lobby scene and spill out onto the sidewalk cafes of the Via Veneto. There are other, quieter hotels in Rome which I prefer, but if your room at the Excelsior is on the top floor front, it will be above the street sounds and will have a balcony and you can sip an evening Campari and watch the sun set gloriously behind St. Peter's dome. I did that once and I will always remember the day. There were flowers in the room from a friend whose card read "Welcome to Roma!" and a motherly chambermaid took my travel-worn clothes to be cleaned at once and huge Turkish towels hung invitingly from a heated rack at the end of an imperial size tub. I'd been in Rome before, but this particular arrival was somehow special, made memorable by a hotel's *caring* environment.

The Japanese are sometimes criticized for trying too hard to imitate American service and facilities in their modern hotels. It's true, they do a remarkably authentic U.S.-style job with breakfast: fresh orange juice, scrambled eggs and plenty of *Kerroggs.* If you've ever done time in a true sleep-on-the-floor Japanese *ryokan,* however, (with fish goodies for breakfast) you will probably welcome any Japanese efforts to be "western."

The late, great Imperial Hotel in Tokyo, the one Frank Lloyd Wright designed in the Twenties to be earthquake-proof, was one of the best. By the time I was a guest, the quaint old Imperial had survived both earthquakes and war and, probably as a consequence, the stone floors of its corridors were as uneven as the ruins of a Greek temple. Nevertheless, it still stood, not only as a memorial to a great architect, but as a hotel which had a unique personality and a staff that really understood hospitality.

The only thing the Imperial couldn't survive was the passage of time. I'm glad I enjoyed it before they tore it down. (P.S., there's a fine new Imperial on the same site in Tokyo today. It has a cavernous lobby and vast, contemporary proportions, but the ghost of Frank Lloyd Wright lingers only in a small bar where the decor of the old hotel has been duplicated.)

Today, I like the Otani in Tokyo well enough. It may have its trite "international" features, like a revolving bar-restaurant on top, but it also has some original Japanese touches. They wake you in the morning with taped, piped-in sounds of birds chirping. There are also stern admonitions posted: no cooking or open fires allowed in the rooms or hallways. In other words, make yourself at home, by all means, but don't carry it too far!

There was a fall day I remember some years ago, one of life's perfect days I should say, when English friends invited us to drive out of London with them, just a leisurely afternoon in the Alvis with a first stop at the great meadow of Runnymede where the Magna Carta was signed in 1215 and where a monument to our John Kennedy now looks down on the green fields. We went on to have tea and Hovis bread in Oxford in late afternoon and then, at about sundown, we came to that English inn which will always be *all* English inns in my affections, the ancient and honorable George at Dorchester-on-Thames. Of course, it was the warmth of the occasion as well as the place, but the George's great hearth was crackling with hospitality that night and other travelers from the road were gathering around the bar as darkness settled outside. The chicken Kiev was the best I've ever eaten and the wine was cool and I felt myself almost literally enfolded by the protection of the grand old coaching inn. This was, indeed, being "looked after" in the original and best sense of the term.

A few years later, Karen and I stopped at the George again, to be welcomed like old friends. This time they gave us the Vicar's room, canopied bed, half-timbers and all. Next morning early we were packed to leave, but there was no one about to accept our payment. I left a note asking that our bill be forwarded to my Connecticut address and, a month or so later, a statement arrived from the George—with apologies for the inconvenience and an invitation to be sure and come again.

In the last 25 years, the big international hotels have added a lot of show business to their hospitality, but it is sometimes a poor substitute for personal caring. At one of the major international hotels in Beirut, a costumed "Arab" roams the lobby in unlikely pantaloons, carrying an ornate Arabian coffee pot and a stack of small cups which he clicks in his palm-like castinets. Over and over, he repeats the unctuous phrase, "You are welcome . . . You are welcome . . ." but if you've just been ripped off between the airport and the hotel by a real Arab cab driver (without pantaloons) you don't feel very welcome or very well looked after either.

I prefer the more humble greeting of the young novice monk a Koyasan, Japan, who wore a baseball jacket and personally carried my bags into the monastery dormitory because he was the entire staff and he was going to take good care of his American guest. I even remember with a certain sympathy the depressing honesty of the plywood motel called the Gateway on Majuro in the Marshall Islands. On the day I arrived, the manager had just had his first telephone installed and he spent the afternoon calling all the other people on the island who also had phones. He didn't bother to announce that I was welcome, but he said if we needed anything at the other end of the island, we could use his pickup truck.

Skylodge in Nadi, Fiji, was not a place which looked after guests with any cosmopolitan elan, but it had a certain way about it all the same. There was a bar girl from Tonga who may or may not have been a member of the staff, but who did her best to make guests feel welcome. She said she had a lot of children by a lot of fathers and added a little wistfully that none of these men ever came back to see their kids. She liked to dance to the drum-heavy rhythms of the hotel's own combo, four fat Fijians who called themselves the Bula Boys.

On Saturday night, Skylodge was the only action spot in town: a bamboo bandstand, colored lights and a dance floor overflowing with swaying bodies, some of them still dressed in airline uniforms, some wearing hardhats belonging to the nearby goldmine, big Fiji men in skirts and girls in muumus with hibiscus blossoms pressed into fuzzy hair. "Over this ear means you're looking," the girl from Tonga explained.

After a few days stay at Skylodge, the guest becomes a personal friend of the establishment and will probably be addressed by his first name.

"You should try dancing in bare feet and a Fiji skirt, Charles," I was advised by one of the boys of the staff. He was a young 200-pounder who said he sometimes sailed his own one-man canoe a few hundred miles to his home island in the archipelago.

"Okay," I said, thinking of the girl from Tonga, "but where do I get one?"

"I take you shopping with me," the young Fijian offered and that afternoon we went to an Indian dry goods shop in town and selected a man's wraparound skirt with a blue and white pattern. It was secured around the waist with a knot.

"Do you wear underwear with these?" I asked, thinking that a pin would be a more secure way of keeping the skirt on.

"No underwear unless you are afraid," my friend said with a laugh. "No one in Fiji afraid," he added.

It seemed to me at the time that all this was a service which one might not expect in most hotels.

Near the rim of Ngorongoro Crater there is a lodge, a hotel if you will, where, on one of my visits, a very black chef made excellent early morning pancakes and a young manager with a British colonial manner made the rounds of the dining room to be sure his guests all had their box lunches for the trip into the crater. He said he wanted to manage a hotel in London someday, but right now he was making the best of Tanzania. I watched him checking the box lunches, cracking open some of the hard boiled eggs to be sure they were done enough and making certain that the salt and pepper packets would not spill into the chocolate cake. I was impressed. Even in remote Africa, even in serving a box lunch, a dedicated *hôtelier* can find many ways to take proper care of people, I thought.

There is an open-air pool and rooftop restaurant at the summit of the Singapore Hilton and on a hot night a mild breeze comes off the city and the harbor beyond. It can carry the smell of the sea, of food cooking, of joss burning, of the Orient. Singapore's lights twinkle through the darkness like a moving carnival, but the sounds of hawkers or mah-jongg are muted and distant because the hotel stands tall above the streets, a sort of self-contained environment of its own, a life-support system for a traveler.

Hiltons and other large American hotel chains are sometimes criticized for being just this—a sort of security cocoon for Americans abroad, a place where they can get their hamburgers and their martinis without having to mingle too intimately with the natives. Well enough, that may be true, but what's wrong with a feeling of security after all? I've stayed in Hiltons here and there around the world, not consistently, but enough to know that they are usually well run and often far better in their services than that "cute little place just off the main square," which may be an indifferent dump. Naturally, any 1000-room hotel is going to be somewhat perfunctory to the individual guest, at least until he asks for something. But when a Hilton

—or Sheraton or Intercontinental—guest *does* demand to be looked after in some particular, he usually gets very expert attention.

Not every hotel I can remember has provided that essential sense of security. On the island of Syros in the Aegean, the management of the small Hotel Hermes seemed much more anxious to please the local constabulary than to guarantee my rest. It was a few years ago when the colonels were running things in Greece. The phone rang in my room in the middle of the night and the voice said that I was wanted by the police.

"You must come now," were the final words before I heard the disconnect. The alternative, I thought, was that they would probably come and get me. No amount of flashing the receiver button could get anyone to come back on the line with an explanation.

Absurd, I thought, but I pulled on pants, shirt and shoes and made my way down empty halls and stairs to the front desk. A young man of about 15 who was probably honored with the title of night manager was waiting for me. I grumbled at him. He pointed wordlessly out the front door. Not far down the waterfront I saw a pair of green lights on a building and a police car parked in front. Night Manager nodded. That's where I should go. Apparently it was voluntary, I was still technically a free man—but not free enough to go back to bed.

Of course it was all a mistake. The Greek cops—or were they soldiers?—had a radio message for some traveling American. Any American would do, apparently, even at 2 A.M. and since I may have been the only American on the island that night, the Hotel Hermes wasn't about to stand in the way of the authorities.

There is no police-state authority on Koror in the Western Carolines, but there is a hideaway hotel there, down the jungle road from the ruins of a Japanese temple. I shall remember it always as the place where the manager gave me his shoes.

In the last 25 years, hotels have ventured into a lot of remote places, bringing U.S.-style amenities to what used to be only safari country. The Koror Continental clings to the hillside overlooking a pocket bay and some of the famed Rock Islands. It is a young, modern place of 52 rooms, each with a balcony and a view that makes you feel that you alone have discovered Paradise. Manager Hank Hickox doesn't have much time for the beauties of nature, however. He has problems finding enough fresh meat and milk for his kitchen and enough electricity and fresh water for the guest rooms. Koror is one of those places where a Jeep, a short wave radio, full scuba tanks, a good diesel mechanic and the every-other-day Air Micronesia flight from Guam are the essentials of survival. Making the guest feel that all this is no problem and that he will be well looked after, come what may, is part of the manager's task.

One night at dinner, Hickox asked if I'd ever read Herman Wouk's novel, *Don't Stop the Carnival*. "It's all about the kind of damn fool who would try to run a hotel in a dead-end of the world." Outside the dining room, the rain came down as if someone had knifed the clouds' bellies. There were only about six guests in the hotel.

"Going to see our movie tonight?" Hickox asked after coffee.

"You have movies—here?"

"It's always the same one," he said apologetically, "but not many of our guests stay long enough to notice."

Later we sat around the small lobby and listened to the rain and watched divers explore Truk lagoon on a sheet pinned to the wall. In the middle of the film, Hickox tapped me on the shoulder and handed me a pair of his old sneakers. "These are what you'll need tomorrow for walking on the reef," he whispered.

I thought that was very personal service.

It's funny how remembering one hotel brings back another until they all seem to come rushing back out of a quarter century on the road. I remember one round-the-world trip Karen and I made when we stayed in 30 hotels in 90 days. Some were lost in the blur, but some stand out for one reason or another.

The Kandara Palace in Jiddah, Saudi Arabia, for example. The lobby was full of Swiss, Japanese, Australians, Dutch and every other nationality of businessmen, all of them hoping to sell something to the oil-rich Arabs. It was a reasonably well run place in a surly sort of way, but I noticed that the walls of my room were splotched here and there with blood. Before the night was over I understood that this was evidence of battles which previous guests had fought with the giant Red Sea mosquitos which entered the unscreened windows.

In the dining room of the Kandara, a hungry American's eyes might find "scrambled eggs and sausage" on the breakfast menu, but, alas, in Moslem Arabia, the "sausage" turns out to be a non-pork frankfurter—just as the Kandara "bar" turns out to be a nice place to drink Perrier on the rocks. It isn't that they don't want to cater to a guest's every need in Arabia, it's just that sometimes the Koran forbids.

At the Old Ground Hotel in Ennis, Ireland, the bar is, as it should be, a healing place and as good a spot as I know to make critical evaluations of local malts. Not much need be said for the Old Ground's capacity to make guests feel at home. Like Ireland itself, it is an establishment run with a proper caring, the sort of place which, when one's wanderings are done, might be remembered longest and best. The peat fire in the lobby always took the chill off the evening and the Irish oatmeal was a good way to begin each day.

Which brings me to the question people eventually ask:

"What's your favorite hotel?" I've often thought about that myself and have usually concluded that there can be no final or arbitrary answer . . . it always depends. I want to go back to the Sheraton at Kaanapali some day when it's a beach and a rest I'm looking for. Or to the fine old Shelburne in Dublin if I'm in the mood for pubs. Or to the Moskva Pupp at Carlsbad in Czechoslovakia for the flavor of the Hapsburg days. Or to the Hermitage in Monte Carlo to look down on the most colorful motor race in the world. There are also great hotels I've not yet seen and maybe one of these will occupy a favorite place in my memory some day. For the moment, however, there *is* a hotel, and a place, which, if I had but one more ticket to buy, would be my choice.

The Mandarin, hard by Hong Kong's storybook harbor, is not an old establishment as great hotels go. I remember when it was only an idea less than 15 years ago. When it became a reality, I thought it the most beautiful and tasteful hotel. But now that I've been a Mandarin guest a number of times over a number of years, I realize that it isn't just the Venetian glass chandeliers and golden temple carvings in the lobby, or the 14 languages and 3 Chinese dialects spoken by the staff, or the Dutch veal and Hokkaido salmon and grouse from Scotland that are so important after all—nor even the Swedish teakwood coathangars, 700 coil springs in every mattress, Rolls-Royce airport service, Irish linen sheets, staff of 1100 (about 2 per guest!) and year-'round fresh strawberries. It is the feeling that every hotel worthy of the name must somehow project if it is to be anything more than a rooming house—yes, the feeling of being "looked after."

You'll see what I mean someday when a typhoon comes across the China Sea and lashes Hong Kong and your hotel becomes, briefly, a refuge. Printed instructions given to guests at these times explain that there is no need to worry, old chap, "the Mandarin roomboys have been trained to cope with such situations. They will bolt your balcony door, close the venetian blinds and draw the curtains . . . If Signal No. 9 is hoisted, the Harbour Room, Lookout Bar and the Man Wah restaurant on the Top Floor will close and, instead, meals will be served in the Connaught Room on the First Floor.

"There will be music and dancing with dinner as usual, how-ever . . ."

♦   ♦   ♦

That's my kind of hotel.

CHAPTER 15
Tall Tales from Down Under

THE ROAD FROM Darwin to Alice Springs is called the Stuart Highway on the maps of Australia, but people in the Northern Territory call it simply "the track." There is a pub about every 80 miles, functional establishments which, by law, must remain open 24 hours to attend to the needs of travelers and their vehicles. "Tank and tummy stations" they're called.

There are also a few settlements along the route—Katherine, Daly Waters, Tennant Creek, names like that, and in each there is a police station and jail kept by a resident constable and a native boy who is usually called the black tracker because of his skills at following a trail.

We had come several hundred miles down the track in a police van to pick up some prisoners for return to Darwin. Ten-day jail sentences, usually for drunkenness, can be served in the small police lock-ups, but more serious offenders and longer terms must be brought back to the big city at the "top end" of the track. ("Alice" is the "bottom end.")

The prisoners, four of them, were being held at Daly Waters

in a clean, modern lock-up that was like an outdoor cage in a zoo. Three of the men were aborigines, one was white. They had been tried in a circuit court, found guilty of various thefts and assaults. They were a good natured lot and the police dealt with them like old friends on a first name basis.

Just before everyone piled into the van for the first leg of the trip north, a little band of local "abos" arrived to play a parting musical concert for their jail-bound friends. One of them carried Australia's ubiquitous native wind instrument, the didgerydoo, a bazooka-size length of pipe or hollow wood which emits a mournful moan. It is accompanied by the rhythm of clicking sticks, pieces of iron-hard wood which ring when struck together.

The stick players, Mickey Rooney and Number Two George, were also vocalists, groaning notes to accompany Billy Brown on the didgerydoo.

Two or three selections were played after the group had found a shady spot in which to sit on the ground. The pieces seemed to differ only in tempo. When they were done, the players and the prisoners said goodbye and we all got into the truck, prisoners in the back and the police officer and me up front. A small window covered with steel mesh separated the good guys from the bad guys.

After about two miles on the road, a terrible odor came from the rear of the van.

"Happens every time," said the constable, shaking his head in despair.

"What happens?" I asked, opening my vent window wider.

"Bowel movement," said the constable, as if he were giving proper testimony in court. "One of those abos back there has probably never ridden in a motorcar before and he's scared to death, so he's let go in his pants. Happens every damn time."

It was a long 80 miles to the next pub and some beer for us and some buckets of water for the back of the van.

◆   ◆   ◆

I had come to Australia to write a story about the black trackers, that small group of legendary aborigines who are attached to police stations, particularly in the Northern Territory, and who are supposed to have an almost supernatural skill at following a trail, animal or human.

The Northern Territory is a half million square miles of hostile country where criminals are hard to run down and people who "go bush" and get lost are advised that they may prolong their survival by eating hornets' larvae or sucking water out of the stomachs of frogs. It's rough country and there can be any number of reasons for organizing search parties.

"What can you tell me about your trackers?" I asked Constable Bob Hayden when we were refreshed, deodorized and back on the road again. "Are they really as good as the stories say?"

Hayden just smiled. "It's like anything else," he said in a broad Aussie accent, not taking his eyes off the road. "There's good and there's bad. We've got a couple of blokes up in Darwin who couldn't track an elephant through the mud. But most abos are good at it and some are exceptional. You're going to meet a pretty good one at this next station."

The Holden van sped along the track, only a narrow road, its gravelly surface grinding dryly under the tires. We left a trail of red dust behind. An hour could pass without seeing another car moving in either direction. On both sides of the track was lightly wooded bush country with a few dry riverbeds, giant anthills, plenty of eucalyptus and other gum trees and some palmetto. Once in a while I saw a kangaroo or a big lizard.

The tracker at the next station was called Jim. Police Constable Kevin Smith gave him permission to talk with me. "It's all right, Jim," he said, "tell the Yank what you do."

Jim was about 6-2, 26 years old. He wore the same khakis as his boss, the same digger hat, the same badge. But the white man's uniform fitted him like a gunnysack.

"He's a good boy," Smith said, using a tone which went out of style long ago in America. "He's a little young to be a really great tracker yet, but he's a good man to back you up if you run into strife."

"Strife" in the Northern Territory can be a spear or a knife or a broken bottle. Jim didn't really look like he was ready for combat, nor was there anything about him that suggested any supernatural powers either. He was shy as a child. He gave me a broad, white smile, looked down at his feet and said nothing.

This tracking is probably a myth, I thought. Like using a forked stick to find water . . .

After a few moments of embarrassed silence, Jim excused himself to go help transfer the prisoners from the van to the jail for overnight. The two constables caught up on all the news from up and down the track, both personal and official. The few dozen officers stationed at the small settlements along the track are usually married and live with their families, either in the same building with the jail–courthouse or at least next door in a sort of law enforcement compound. The policeman's wife prepares meals for prisoners when necessary. The houses are modern, simple and often built up off the ground on columns to provide better cooling in the heat, less dampness in the wet and protection from whatever wild creatures might come out of the bush after dark.

We sat up late that night. A slight breeze came through the screens, bringing with it the smell of woodsmoke sweet as perfume. Smith and his wife and Hayden and myself were around the kitchen table, opening beers and talking about the trackers.

I wanted to know how much was legend, how much fact.

"It's not a legend when I take my native boy out in the bush and in only a few minutes he cuts [finds] a track that's three weeks old! I've *seen* that, mate!" Smith was doing what he liked best: drinking beer and talking about police work.

Hayden cited history. "Some of them have been famous, you know. Black Syd, for example, and Smiler and Old Charlie. They were known all over Australia. Sometimes they tracked fugitives a thousand miles. They can tell whether the man they're following is weak or strong. They can tell his age, his height, his weight and what he eats. No good walking backwards to fool them, either. That's an old trick to an abo."

They were double teaming me now, two amiable cops, each trying to impress a Yank guest with good stories. Smith said a good tracker could follow a man's footprints faster than he made them. "My Jim doesn't look *down* at tracks. His eyes look about 12 feet in front of him and he moves ahead fast, breaking into a run sometimes, leapfrogging ahead to pick up the trail farther on. There's no getting away from him."

"They've been trained to see everything," said Hayden. "It's usually their mothers, the old gins, who taught them when they were kids. People think it's plain old footprints they follow, but it's not. It's *signs.* That's how they can track you over hard ground and stone. Maybe they'll see the body of an ant you stepped on an hour ago. If you climb a tree, they'll look for hair off your legs. If you go in the water, they'll look for oils off your skin."

And what happens, I asked, when it's a native being tracked by a native?

"Those are the best chases," Hayden said. "Abo against abo, each trying to outwit the other. They each know how to live off the bush for months at a time. They each know what the other is thinking . . ."

In Australia's courts, evidence from a police tracker is taken as from an expert witness. Smith explained. "My Jim stands up to the judge and he says, 'I am a native boy. I was born at such and such a place 26 years ago. My father teach me to track. I went to the oasis last Tuesday with Constable Smith. I see a track on the dirt. It had little cuts on the front of the left boot. The boot was worn down on outside. I'd know that track anywhere.'

"Then the judge tells the suspect to walk and Jim studies the track," Smith went on. "There's no hesitation about it. If he says, 'I see that feller walk today. He is the same one . . .' then the bloke's as good as convicted."

◆ ◆ ◆

About 11 o'clock, Smith turned an ear to catch some sounds on the night air. "Movie's over," he said. Once a week there is an outdoor movie in a recreation area near the settlement. I heard some laughter and shouts in the distance, but there was nothing but darkness beyond the screens.

"Sometimes we have a little strife after the picture," Smith said. He was folding up a beer can neatly with his fingers. "The abos are excited by movies. Sometimes they set fire to the bush just for the hell of it when its over. Sometimes there's a spearing or two . . ." Nobody around the table seemed to take the statement as unusual.

"But I wouldn't want you to get the idea that this is a lawless area," Hayden said. "Not much trouble along this track, really, except when some of the lads has a few too many flagons of plonk."

Downstairs, by the courthouse door, I had seen a display of wanted posters. Three were for murder. There was a reward of $2000 for information.

Jim came in about midnight. He had been at the movie. Smith asked him about the disturbance. Jim said it was

" 'nother boy" who had started it.

Smith asked, "Which way all about 'nother black boy?"

Jim answered, "Him bin go that way," pointing in the direction with his lips puckered out.

"You all gottem plenty bush tucker, Jim?" Smith asked, apparently changing the subject.

Jim said no, no more plenty, just a little bit. Tucker means food; Jim was being baited for more information about the troublemaker at the movies.

"Anybody else bin come up this place, makem trouble?"

"No more," said Jim. Then he added, "Me all about sit down meself." Whatever that meant, Smith understood.

"Well, when all about 'nother black boy comes back, you tellim, suppose policeman go movie picture 'bout next week." Smith was speaking another language, the words coming out quickly.

"All right," said Jim. "We tellim all about."

Now Smith had his reward ready. "You feller gottem plenty tobacco?"

"No more. Nothing."

"All right, Jim. You all about sit down and I'll gibbit you tobacco and tucker."

Jim sat down in the kitchen and his eyes moved over all the empty beer cans and he gave me the same big smile as when we met, but he didn't speak again until Smith came back with a bag of groceries and tobacco for him.

After Jim said thank you and left, Smith told a story about him.

"He brought us some wild honey a while ago and it was a surprise because I didn't know there were any bees near here. I asked him how he found the honey and he said he had tracked a bee.

" 'Tracked a *bee?*' I said to him. 'You'll have to show me how you do that or I'll think you stole this honey, Jim!'

"Well, he took me out into the bush, not far, and we came to a place where he stopped and stood very still listening.

" 'Mine tinkit I bin find somethin' 'bout here,' he said, and pretty soon he spotted a bee flying and he watched it settle on some wildflowers. Very carefully, he crept up on the bee and caught it in his hand the way you'd take a quick swipe at a fly. He gave me a big smile, all the while still holding the bee in his hand.

"I said, 'Fine, Jim, you caught a bee, but that doesn't say how you found the honey.'

"He gestured to follow him to a paw-paw tree and he took some of the sap on one finger and, holding the bee very carefully by its wings, he put a dab of the sap on the bee's underside. Then he came up with a little piece of white down which was about the same size as the bee. Watching me and smiling all the time, he stuck this little feather into the paw-paw sap on the bee's stomach and immediately let it fly off.

"I thought I knew all these abo tricks, but this was a new one on me. There went the bee, buzzing off, but now it was very easy to follow with the naked eye because of that little white feather. Jim gave me one last superior look and took off, *tracking* for honey!"

After that story, we all agreed it was time for bed. I thought about the bee tale for a while before I fell asleep and I finally decided that I would only believe it because I was in Australia.

CHAPTER 16
Fighting the P.C.G.S.

I ONCE KNEW a barber who collected postcards sent to him by customers when they traveled. He displayed the cards around four sides of the mirror in his shop. Another collection was Scotch-taped to the cash register. And he had a special department for holy postcards from Rome—the Vatican, the Pope, the Sistine Chapel, various Madonnas, etc. Whenever Sal knew I was about to leave on a trip, he would always warn me, "Don't forget to send a card!" And I usually remembered, because to come home without having added something to the collection was to risk the possibility of Sal's heartfelt disappointment.

"You were in Liechtenstein and you didn't send me a card? I don't *have* one from there!"

Sal was one of the only people I've ever known who truly seemed to care about getting picture postcards from his friends. After many years of travels and much thought about the postcard problem, I have come to the conclusion that, Sal's case notwithstanding, few people feel any need to get a 3½ ✕

160

5½-inch picture of the Matterhorn from me or to learn that the nights are surprisingly cool in Morocco. The whole postcard custom is, I have concluded, a sort of Alphonse and Gaston act: first, I send tangible evidence through the mails that I am thinking of you even in the midst of my revels abroad—and when I come home, *you* show how much this thoughtful gesture meant by telling me it was the best picture of the Matterhorn you've ever seen and what a surprise it was to learn that about Morocco!

Humbug! I am now convinced that the methodical writing of postcards while on a trip is either downright hypocrisy or a slavish giving in to convention. I also think it is a waste of time that could better be spent drinking, a waste of money that might better be spent on whiskey and a waste of good intentions, inasmuch as no one, not even a Florentine cameo carver, can write anything that isn't abbreviated banality in a 2 × 2-inch space.

Having said all that, I must now confess that as a traveler I have sent thousands of postcards over the years and shall probably go on doing so as a sort of reflex. It is only because I have been caught in the postcard trap myself that I feel I can speak as an authority on some aspects of the custom. I am particularly interested in, and distressed by, what I call the P.C.G.S. or Postcard Guilt Syndrome.

Perhaps the oldest cliché about postcards is the one which says that no matter when you mail them, they never get home until after you do. This is usually because we don't write them until the last day of our trip (cliché #2; oh, guilt!) but I also think there is a secret, unwritten agreement among all the postal services of the world to treat postcards as a form of junk mail to be handled with no more dispatch than the stuff addressed "occupant." Even air mail makes no difference. There must be a saying which translates approximately the same from all languages: "Nothing urgent or important is ever written on a postcard."

There is plenty of evidence that this is all too true. Since postcard collecting has become a big hobby, it is possible to browse through countless thousands of old cards which were sent here and there around the world in the last century or more. A study of the personal messages on these cards indicates very quickly that never have so many people had so little to say as those who have written postcards.

Aside from the problem of what to say, one thing that has always given me maddening guilt feelings is trying to select just-right cards for certain people. With Sal the barber it was always easy. He loved pictures of Catholic cathedrals anywhere in the world. My own young children were no problem either. St. Bernard dogs and zoo animals seemed to please them when they were young, but I think I leaned on this taste for too many years. I also continued to print their cards long after they could decipher my longhand.

The precise mating of a postcard to the personality of the recipient is not made any easier by the selection usually afforded. "Views" of mountains and valleys are very big everywhere. So are buildings and monuments. Sailboats on water, flower gardens, main streets at night (after a rain, when the pavement is wet) and folk dancers in costume are also favorites. Postcard subject matter is relentlessly upbeat, happy and sunny. I have been looking for years for a postcard which might show people walking in the rain under umbrellas, or an old abandoned farm, or a strip mine, or even a large prison, but it is apparent that postcards and photo-journalism are still strangers.

One exception to the humdrum nature of the typical postcard

selection is the long-famous but now nearly defunct dirty post-card business. The French were always big in this, so much so that the mere term "French postcard" almost automatically evoked a risqué image. Unfortunately, the sexual revolution in most parts of the globe, save the more advanced Moslem, So-cialist and Third-world nations, has made the average French postcard of yesteryear look like the Sears catalog underwear department. Unfortunately, too, not only has no acceptable adult substitute for the French postcard been developed, but even the old comic-book-style, outhouse-humor cards are being replaced with 3-D novelties and cards that emit the scent of a pine forest when scratched with a fingernail.

Despite the success of the so-called "contemporary," or "stu-dio," or "insult"-type designs in the greeting card industry, the movement hasn't spread to the travel postcard field. Admit-tedly, it's probably hard to be funny about the Matterhorn.

Of course, when and if you find a postcard you like, the one that seems to hit that absolutely nice balance that would suit almost everybody on your list, why not just buy a dozen or 20 *all alike* and be done with it? Is there any reason why everyone back home should get a different card? Should we feel guilty for not having the wit and originality to find something just right for everyone? Uncle Harry may work for the railroad, but are we a better person for sending him a photo of a trestle over the Lower Rhine?

I've always thought that a nice, neutral idea for a card might simply be the flag of the country you are visiting. You could safely send one of those to everybody. It would have its educa-tional benefits, too, inasmuch as most of us don't know the flag of Sweden from the flag of Greece without looking it up. Even Uncle Harry might like this. After all, once you've seen one railroad trestle, you've seen them all.

Also. Do you feel guilty if you write the same "message" on several cards—the same easy combination of words which seems to say it all? Do you feel an obligation to rephrase the message, even if only slightly, for certain people? Are you afraid your friends will compare notes and say, "That's what he wrote to me, too"? If so, these are all signs of the P.C.G.S.

There is a certain false gaity about cards which also troubles me, not only in the pictures, but in the things we write on the other side. The sender might have had the world's worst case of diahrrea the night before, yet he feels obliged to write only some happy variation of the "having a wonderful time" line when he sits down to send greetings the next day. Why else send a card in the first place, after all, if it is not to show that travel is a gay and carefree lark. Even when it isn't—right?

Which brings up another point: aren't postcards really nothing but announcements designed to tell all your friends (who are still presumably stuck at their old postal address) that *you* are traveling again, you lucky schmuck, and where *you* are it is warmer, or cooler, and *so* much more colorful and fascinating than it ever could be back there in the home town. After all, don't most of your friends know you went on this trip in the first place? So why tell them again? Surely not so they will know that you "arrived safely!"

The fact is, if you think about it, cards are not sent to let people know you're thinking of *them;* they're sent so other people will think of you, lucky you, rich you, worldly you, flying-off-again you—up, up and away . . . This, too, contributes to my feelings of guilt.

I am probably doing an injustice to the whole postcard scene, but conscience makes me ask: where is the spontaneity in all this? Where is the honesty? Much as we would like our friends to think that we keep their address and zip code in our head

at all times and then, when overwhelmed with feelings of friendship, we just pluck a card off the rack and send it straight home
from the boat in the underground river, the fact is, we know it
doesn't happen that way. If you're going to send postcards from
a trip, you bring a list with you, you approach the whole thing
the way you face Christmas cards, systematically. Sadly, there
is seldom anything spontaneous about it. If you travel a lot and
send postcards often, you may even find it necessary to make
notations of which cards were sent from where the last time—
i.e., "Sal, Reims cathedral. Uncle Harry, Tower Bridge. Patrick, gnu."

So cynically demanding has the postcard guilt syndrome
become with many travelers, it would not surprise me to learn
that some enterprising concern is cashing in on it. How? With
packets of postcards tailored to wherever you're going, cards
which you can pre-address right at home in advance of your
departure. And why not? We buy packets of foreign money in
advance for convenience. Are not postcards just another travel
obligation which might be simplified or made easier? Some
people buy Christmas cards in July, after all. Do they feel guilty
about it when December comes?

Maybe Hallmark is missing a bet. What would be wrong with
a line of postcards that have greetings already imprinted like
birthday cards or get-well cards? Hallmark copywriters seem to
have zeroed in on the best common-denominator words to use
for almost every occasion, so why not entrust them with our
travel sentiments? These might even turn out to be poetic, like
"I Love Paris in the Springtime . . ." with a picture of Mont-
marte, or even sentimental, "As I travel far from you, this
beautiful valley (substitute: mountain, beach, lake for other
photos) . . . reminds me of our love."

If you are careful, and not too guilt-ridden by the thought,

PDE'ing (pre-departure expediting, that is) of cards could be carried beyond the addressing to the message itself. There are certain phrases which you, as a traveler, are almost bound to use anyway, so you might as well anticipate them in advance. For example, "Marvelous place, but we are still tired after the flight . . ." is no doubt an expression which a survey (if we had one; alas, research in the field is almost non-existent) would rank high among all postcard phrases. It is almost foolproof. So is, "The weather surprised us when we arrived, but it is changing now." Or, "Can't wait to start getting around the country and meeting the real people." You could also safely use, "Our guide is very amusing and full of information about everything." If you feel like grumbling a little, you might prewrite, "The windows in our bus are dirty," or, "The only thing we don't like is the tipping situation."

There is one rather grim risk in pre-writing (PDE'ing, that is) your cards. If you have the misfortune to be on a flight which comes down prematurely, all your friends will know what a fake you were.

Well, I suppose all of this would sound much more learned and my anxieties would seem more solidly based on fact if I only knew how many billions of picture postcards pass through the world's mails each year, and whether the custom is still booming or on the wane. Unfortunately, I have no such statistics, but I suppose the figure may be so great as to be a *prima facie* endorsement of the postcard's eternal popularity and universal appeal. Even if that is so, however, I will not be entirely swayed by mere numbers. After all, I gave up sending Christmas cards several years ago and I've never felt better than when December rolls around each year.

Now if I could just kick this damn postcard habit . . .

CHAPTER 17

Too Good to Put in Coffee

THERE HAS BEEN a lighthouse at Loop Head since 1720, standing on a stony finger of Ireland that points across the Atlantic to America. It was near winter when I found the place, one of those days when the sea wind lifts the gulls almost out of sight and drives the rain into your pockets.

"I can not take you up into the light," the man said in the accent of the west country. "It's because of the bombs and the troubles in the North." He looked at me from under his cap, shaking his head, as if to say it was a pity that an honest-looking American visitor—and one who knew the candlepower of Cape Cod light at that—should have to be refused the traditional hospitality, but that is the way of the world these days.

"We've got two million candles here," he said. "Twenty seven miles they can see us if there's no fog—and when there is, it's a cannon shot every four minutes."

Eventually, of course, after we had looked at the radio equipment and the storage batteries and the clocks, suspicion was gently suspended and we went up into the forbidden tower together. After all, a lighthouse keeper runs out of things to say if he cannot show you his light.

An iron key opened the heavy door and we stepped inside and climbed cold stone stairs, circling up to where the wind thundered against the heavy glass and the great lenses of the light looked out the windows like the eyes of a god.

"It's a day for poteen," the keeper said, looking out at the windblown point of land where the wide mouth of the Shannon meets the Atlantic. He pronounced it *pucheen* and he had a twinkle in his eye when he said it, waiting to see if I knew what he meant.

"Can you distill better whiskey in a storm?" I asked.

"It's not the whiskey, it's the smoke," he laughed. "A good wind takes it away and the smell of the peat with it. No clues for the excise man, if you know what I mean," he said. The twinkle was still there.

"Do they still do it?" I asked. In Dublin, my friend John Ryan had said the making of Irish moonshine was dying out.

"You tell him for me that there's still as much whiskey made out here in these stone cottages as there is fancy stuff with labels on the bottles!"

The 'fancy stuff' is called Jameson's and Power's and Paddy and Tullamore Dew, all different, but all Irish. And, of course, Bushmill's which is made in the North, but there are those in the Republic who will drink it.

Poteen. *Pucheen.* The cold made me think about it. I said I supposed it would be warming, but probably harsh and fiery and full of shillelaghs, what we'd call white lightning at home.

"If that's your misconception," the man said, putting on a touch of injured dignity, "I might change my mind about offering you a ball of malt!"

Ireland. What a lovely place, I thought as we went down the

stairs together like two friends now and headed for the warm interior of a glass.

They've been making whiskey on this island, in stone cottages or proper distilleries, for a thousand years or more, nobody knows how long. As has often been explained, they gave drink its name, *usquebaugh,* water of life. They not only invented the stuff, these Irish, but they went far to perfect it over the centuries. When the English first came invading in 1170, the Irish and whiskey were waiting for them. From then until about 1600, when some Scots like Haig and Dewar and Jameson came over to learn the technique, the Irish had the business all to themselves.

◆ ◆ ◆

In Dublin, fair city, after the pubs close at 11 and the last of the crowd has left the Bailey where Behan did some of his drinking and where they keep the front door from James Joyce's house preserved like a museum piece, you walk home on quiet streets and the smell of barley malt drifts through the mist like incense in whiskey's own cathedral.

"If it's not Guinness's malt, it's ours," John Ryan says. "It's always in the air. Don't notice it any more myself."

Malt is a sweet smell, full of promises, natural rather than industrial, and at Power's distillery on John's Lane, the scent is so heavy you wonder why no one there mentions it as they would a particularly heavy fog.

They've been making whiskey at this odd jumble of brick buildings and smokestacks since 1791. The place could almost be a museum, a glimpse into the way things once were. Sir James Talbot Power's velocipede still hangs on the wall in the courtyard and a 1904 sign warns workers not to dump their tea leaves in the drinking fountain. Stair treads leading up to the board room are edged in gleaming brass and on the dark walls, around the big table, stern portraits of the Powers look down: Sir John, Sir James, Sir Thomas. There is a huge old Glasgow-built steam engine that once supplied all the distillery's power. Alas, it is fired up only once a year now, but even that is a defiant act, a token of the fact that while many things may change, some things don't—and Power's Gold Label never will.

◆ ◆ ◆

On the way home from the lighthouse, I stopped at Keating's New Bar in Kilbaha. The establishment offers bed and breakfast for an Irish pound ($2.30) and claims to be the westernmost licensed premises in Ireland. Actually, Patrick Keating wouldn't say "westernmost." The man just doesn't talk like that. He has a sign painted on the outside of the building which declares that of all the pubs in Ireland, it's his which is closest to New York. There is a childish drawing of a jetliner headed for the skyscrapers. Emigration. Still the dream.

Pat and another gentleman who was wearing many sweaters were watching a London horseshow on the telly when I came in from the storm. There was a pause while the three of us watched a particular horse and rider make their way over a series of jumps without mishap. Then.

"A whiskey, please," I said.

"Powers?"

"No," I said, "I'll try a Paddy."

"You're not from around here," Keating said pleasantly enough. "People around here are loyal to their own drop."

"And what might that be?"

"Powers, usually," he said, turning to me with the glass. "Paddy's a Cork whiskey," he added without prejudice.

"How many people live in Kilbaha?" I said.

He was watching the horseshow again and drying glasses at the same time. Another rider made it over the jumps before Pat returned to my question.

"A hundred?" I prompted.

"Well, let's see. There's about 20 houses between here and the light, that's all."

"Anybody make *pucheen* out here?"

Pat Keating smiled. "Aye," he said, "on windy days."

◆ ◆ ◆

For those with an idea that in an industrial age all whiskey is just whiskey, consider the Irish method. Whether it's made on a windy day in a cottage or in a law-abiding, tax-paying firm, it begins with the aforementioned barley grain, about half of which has been allowed to sprout and then dried into the form called malt. This is ground into a mash and mixed with hot water to produce a sweetish "worts."

In 80 hours, with the help of yeast, the worts ferments to become a strong beer of about 8 percent alcohol. It's called "wash."

"It's what happens next that makes all the difference," John Ryan said—a three-stage distillation of the wash in great copper pot stills, one batch and 13 hours at a time. From "low wines," to "feints," to "new whiskey," the process goes, reducing the original wash by more than 90 percent. Then, clear as spring water, it spills forth at 190 proof under the watchful eye of the excise man, headed for at least 5 years of aging in old sherry hogsheads or rum or bourbon barrels.

How does this make Irish whiskey different? The three distillations are unique, but the taste? It's not peat-flavored Scotch, nor Canadian rye, and certainly not corn-fed American. Irish has a style of its own. "It's what Scotch drinkers are always hoping for, but never find," I was told. Perhaps. With a fairly consistent sampling program, I was beginning to identify, to define. But I could still remember the time when I wondered why certain of my drinking friends made such a loyal fuss over their "Irish."

◆   ◆   ◆

Sgt. Joseph A. Carr was an Irishman from the Marble Hill section of New York. The night we went overseas, Joe and I and some other GIs were waiting for our troop train to pull into the station at Newark, N.J. None of us knew where we were going and the anxiety of this made Joe consider the purchase of a last stateside bottle, one for the road, as it were.

When the train arrived there was a great groaning up of barracks bags onto shoulders and helmets clattering against carbines—and then an awful crash. Joe's bottle had splintered on the station platform. A dark stain spread quickly onto the concrete and a glorious aroma wafted up through the chill air, bringing wistful smiles to all our faces, all but Joe's.

"You fuckers don't understand," he said. "It wasn't just whiskey. It was *Irish* whiskey!"

It was true; I didn't understand. I just had an idea the stuff was strong. I didn't know it was special.

A lot of people still have the idea that Irish whiskey is strong, something to put in Irish coffee or drink down before having a tooth extracted. But before Prohibition, Americans drank more Irish whiskey than any other flavor—there were 400 brands on the American market—and there were no complaints. Unfortunately, during the Great Drought, some very bad imitations of Irish were assembled in bathtubs here and there and when the day came that alcohol was legal again in the U.S., fathers told their sons to be sure and drink only "good whiskey." They didn't mean Irish.

◆   ◆   ◆

Prohibition wasn't just an American idea. On Patrick Street in Cork there is a monument to Father Mathew, a Capuchin monk, "the father of temperance," who would have brought Prohibition to Ireland as if the idea were not too absurd to contemplate. It speaks well for the temperance of the Irish that the monument still stands, for Cork is a drinking man's town, a city of steep, San Francisco streets, many of them lined shoulder to shoulder with the hundreds of pubs for which the city is famous.

Wise's distillery, on the River Lee in Cork, burned in 1918 and its stark ruins stand next to warehouses that survived and are still used to house whiskey. John Hyde is there, a courtly and silver-haired gentleman who says he remembers the fire, which is a long time to be in the whiskey business.

"Mr. Wise was very strict," he says. "He hated the excise man as much as any of us, but he'd allow no cheating, none at all. 'The whiskey business is an honorable business,' he'd say and that would be the end of it."

Wise and James Murphy and two others had merged into Cork Distillers in 1869. They are still making whiskey at the old flax mill where Murphy started in 1827, still using water power and the biggest pot still in the world, a goose-necked copper giant that holds 31,000 gallons.

In Cork, you begin to understand that Irish whiskey takes some of its flavor from more than barley.

♦   ♦   ♦

Like Murphy and Wise in Cork, John Jameson prospered in Dublin. "We make the best whiskey in the world and we will be pleased to take your order," was the extent of his marketing philosophy. Even when changing tastes in the American market toppled Irish whiskey from the top to the bottom, Irish traditionalists were loathe to do anything about their "strong, heavy" product. Would Yeats rewrite his poems for the critics? Would Shaw shave his beard!

Meantime, the Scots promoted lightness and outsold Irish 100 to 1.

By 1969, the Irish distillers, now merged again into a last-ditch union, decided they'd heard enough about how popular Irish coffee was becoming and made plans to go after the drinking man's market.

"Our stuff is just too good to put in coffee," they said and with the help of American taste experts they came up with a new blend calculated to be "even more acceptable to a Scotch drinker than Scotch."

If it works, they're going to sell a lot of whiskey and they're going to need a lot of production.

◆　◆　◆

"It's like an old relative who is slowly dying," says young Barry O'Mahoney. "Sooner or later you have to consider euthanasia."

O'Mahoney is talking about the old days and the old ways. He is helping Irish Distillers get their big new "production facility" at Midleton ready to make the new whiskey for the world markets. When it's finished this year (1975) it will be the first new distillery built in Ireland in 200 years. It will be able to produce 4.3 million gallons a year. All of Ireland's old pot stills combined can only turn out 2.9 million gallons today.

"And some of those old pot stills really have to be coaxed and pampered," O'Mahoney says, not looking much like a distiller in his construction-site hard hat. "It only takes a difference of a degree or two in temperature and you produce lousy alcohol, you know," he says, "and if an old pot like that big one at Murphy's should burst it would be the equivalent of a vascular hemorrhage in an old person."

It is the kind of thing you wouldn't say if you thought the old person was listening.

Although O'Mahoney sounds like an efficiency expert and although Midleton looks like a factory, oldtimers in the business say the new plant is located in the middle of the finest barley region in Ireland, that the water is the very same source that Murphy used for a century or more, that the triple-distilled process will never be altered, that the stills are made from the very same grade of copper as before. The only difference is that in the new plant, 11 men will be doing what it now takes 70 to do in the old distilleries.

If you acquire a taste for Irish whiskey, I thought, the best thing about Midleton is that there will be no shortage; you can remain loyal to your own drop.

CHAPTER 18
Don't Shoot!

I TAKE PICTURES when I travel. I *like* to take pictures. I have probably failed more often than I have succeeded in making great or memorable shots, but photography has added a dimension to my adventures all the same. It has gotten me up early in the morning to catch that certain light and led me to chase elusive sunsets from Dharhan to Domme. My camera has been a valid excuse to focus on a lot of pretty girls as well as an *open sesame* to places where a writer might be excluded (and where only fools and photographers would want to perch).

There is no fairness doctrine in the way writers and photographers are dealt with by those in authority. Sometimes a photographer is allowed in vantage spots which a writer would envy —but often a cameraman is denied opportunities to make pictures which a writer is left free to paint with words.

My sympathy is with the photographer. Usually he has but one chance to make his picture. He dies a thousand anxious deaths before he knows he has succeeded. And he suffers a thousand indignities because he works with a machine that is sometimes despised, often feared, occasionally smashed and never really trusted or understood.

Furthermore, I've seen a great many NO PHOTOGRAPHY signs around the world, but I have yet to see one which says NO WRITING.

Picture prohibitions turn up in an ill-assorted lot of places: topless nightclubs, the Vatican, pre-historic caves in France, certain museums and waxworks, American Indian rain dances, Buddhist spirit painting sessions, roulette casinos, Polaris submarines, mental hospitals, automobile proving grounds, America's Cup yachts, etc. Of course, there's often a reason for secrecy, even if not always very well-articulated, but even so, censorship is more often directed at the photographer than the writer.

The camera's problem is not just that it sees, but that it remembers so well. It keeps. We "take" a picture. Since the coming of the Polaroids, of course, the camera can give a picture back and instantly too, and this may occasionally help a photographer out of a jam. Nevertheless, there are still too many NO PHOTOGRAPHY signs.

Take the Tower of London, for example, where the Beefeater guards will gladly pose as stiffly as gin bottles for tourist cameras, but where pictures of the crown jewels are off limits. Since these baubles are what most people have come to see, many visitors resent the rule. As if to help enforce it, the lighting in the jewel room is so poor that if you can't hand-hold 1/15th of a second exposure wide open, you haven't a chance. The guards, perhaps lulled by the gloom, ignore the sounds of clicking shutters.

At the Egyptian Museum in Cairo, they are more strict. No cameras. Absolutely. Signs everywhere. The Arab vendors who hover around the entrance displaying thousands of plastic mounted slides for sale apparently control the concession. If they see a tourist entering the museum with a casually concealed camera, they report him to the guards who act at once. The guards seem afraid of the Arabs who sell the pictures.

The last time I was there, dutifully cameraless, I was stopped by a guard in the room where King Tut's golden coffin reposes in all its glory—and in pretty good light.

"American?" the guard said.

I said yes.

"Take picture?"

"Of course not!" I answered defensively.

He stepped confidentially closer. "You *want* to take picture?"

"What? Without a camera?" I said, somewhat indignant. Why didn't they tell me that even though no cameras were allowed, I should bring one anyway?

The guard pointed to a sort of stubby stepladder which he kept in a corner of the room. "For picture?" he said, not yet believing that this American didn't have a camera hidden somewhere on his person. When he finally saw that I was clean he seemed disappointed, but offered the use of the stepladder anyway.

It did afford a better look at Tut—but I didn't give the guard any tip for using it.

St. Peter's, in Vatican City, used to take a no-nonsense approach to their no-photography rule. A young cleric took your camera at the door, checked it free of charge and returned it to you when you left. As the world population of cameras exploded however and as they became more and more pocket-sized, the checking system broke down. Only the NO PHOTOGRAPHY signs remain.

The sound of camera shutters is pretty much lost within the

cavernous interior of the huge basilica, but the bluish blinks of flashbulbs are constantly visible. In front of the now-restored and newly protected Pieta, the church that allows no photography has thoughtfully provided a small wastebasket for used flash cubes, film wrappings and Polaroid trash.

Meaningless NO PHOTOGRAPHY signs left in places where photography is nevertheless tolerated may be a misleading nuisance, but I think they are preferable to those situations where there are no signs but where photography truly *is* forbidden. This can result in some nasty surprises.

East Berlin in the early 1960s was a tension spot. Tanks and armored vehicles were drawn up on both sides of Checkpoint Charlie. Tourists were being bussed into the Communist zone on tours, but if one had an American passport there was nothing to stop an individual tourist from just walking into the east zone—except perhaps common sense.

You passed the *You-are-leaving-the-American-Zone* signs, followed a zig-zag path through the dragon's teeth tank obstacles and came to *Kontrol.* The day I did it, I carried my camera in full view around my neck.

Two East German policemen, often called Vopos in those days, checked my passport and the amount of money I was carrying and waved me on.

"Can I take pictures in here?" I asked, indicating the camera.

"In the German Democratic Republic, you may photograph anything you like!" The policeman fairly shouted the permission.

"Can I take *your* picture?"

"Nein!"

I walked in and strolled around for most of the afternoon. No tanks in sight. Some Russian soldiers in long overcoats. I took a few pictures of the war ruins. I stopped once and changed film while the soldiers watched me. Obviously, there was nothing to fear.

On my way back through the checkpoint, I was questioned by an American MP who saw the camera around my neck. "Did you take any pictures in there?"

I said I'd photographed street scenes, people, "and that big ruined palace with all the statues, just inside the border."

The MP frowned. "That big ruined place with all the statues is where their tanks are hidden. It is absolutely forbidden to photograph it. Didn't anybody warn you?"

Amazing how dangerous photography can be when nobody puts up a NO PHOTOGRAPHY sign!

In Macau one day, I stood in a park with a group of Chinese who were watching the progress of a game that looked like checkers but wasn't. The two players sat facing each other in silence. The onlookers seemed very respectful of the proceedings. There were quiet comments and mutterings only when moves were made on the board. One of the contestants was an old man with a classic face and a Ho Chi Minh beard. I decided to take his picture.

When my camera shutter disturbed the silence, both players looked at me in what might have been annoyance, but I wasn't sure. In a few minutes, I made another photo from another angle. This proved more than old Ho could bear. He rose from his chair and proceeded to chew me out in Chinese, pointing to the game on the board, shaking his fist and looking to his audience for support. The onlookers mumbled what I feared was agreement. Apparently I had brought bad luck to Ho's game with my evil-eye camera. I backed out in a hurry.

Sometimes I haven't backed out fast enough. In Tel Aviv there is a teeming, noisy market along Carmel Street with everything for sale from antiques to bras to Bedouin rugs. Strolling through the district one afternoon, I happened on a sort of broad alley between two buildings where a group of farm women were plucking chickens. They sat on the ground in a half circle, big piles of fresh-killed, feathered birds on one side and denuded ones on the other. Mountains of white feathers were accumulating and bits of down floated in the air. The women were engaged in a continuous chatter, laughing and making rude gestures while tugging and tearing at the birds. They all rinsed their hands from time to time in cans of water. It certainly looked like a good picture. The light was a little uncertain, but I moved in anyway, camera poised. See the colorful native ladies at work! See the feathers fly! Click!

The colorful native lady closest to me rose at the sound as if she had been launched to the attack. Armed with a half-plucked chicken, she lunged, bringing the soggy bird down on my head. Her shriek of anger was taken up instantly by the others, all of whom now rose from the feathered floor, advancing on me like a ragged army. I made one brief attempt at apology or explanation. Then the contents of one of the cans of rinsing juice hit me.

An Israeli shopkeeper across the street had seen it all and thought it was much funnier than I did. He took me into his shop, gave me a handful of paper towels and interpreted the cries of Hebrew outrage which were still coming from across the street.

"They are saying," he explained, "that you should never photograph a lady when she looks like that."

In most of the developing countries of the so-called Third World, pride in national accomplishments and public works such as airports, war memorials and TV towers is strong indeed. Tour guides in these areas can always tell you just how many gallons of sewage the new treatment plant will handle or

how many million rivets there are in the General Alfonso San-
chez Memorial Bridge. They also think these things should
surely make excellent photographic subjects. And old things,
such as peasants in traditional dress, donkey carts, or the oldest
quarters of the city are often regarded as "not very flattering"
for pictures.

At Jiddah, on the Red Sea, I was arrested one morning by
a Saudi Arabian policeman who caught me photographing a
beautiful old fishing boat, freshly painted in traditional colors,
floating like a mirage in the harbor. Saudi cops are no mirage,
however. They are dressed in army-style khakis, they wear a
beret, carry a rifle and talk tough. I pleaded that it was only a
fishing boat and what could be wrong with a visitor showing his
appreciation for native Arab arts and culture? My companion
that day, an Arab with American citizenship, also pleaded in
vain—and in Arabic.

"This man is doing nothing wrong, officer."

"He is using a camera, isn't he?"

There is no term for camera in Arabic, so the word, sounding
like *kammera,* was sprinkled through the conversation. I
waited. There was much palaver. Eventually, tiring of the
game, and having made us both admit that the fishing boat was
really not worth photographing, the cop let us go.

"Tell your friend to photograph our new water tower," he
said to my Arab friend as we left. "It holds 71 million gallons
and is 150 meters high!"

Sometimes you can take pictures of the "natives," but only
for a price. At a place called Lok Ma Chau, a high point of
ground along the border between Hong Kong's New Territories
and the People's Republic of China, there is a lookout which
has become a favorite tourist stop. In Cold War days, any
glimpse of "China" was a peek into enemy territory. As a result,

bus tours all stopped at the lookout, souvenir stands sprang up full of colorful junk, Coca-Cola and Lowenbrau were available on ice and a platform was constructed, probably by the bus company, for the convenience of tourist photographers who wanted to take a picture through the Bamboo Curtain.

Soon enough, a local Chinese couple turned Lok Ma Chau into a thriving private enterprise for themselves by dressing in the traditional old black pajama outfits worn by peasants of another era and posing for pictures against the grim backdrop of Communism. They wore straw sandals and coolie hats and played the roles of *Good Earth* Chinese to the hilt.

"Dollah, dollah," they chant their fee at every tourist with a camera—but just try to get their faces exposed on film without paying! Both can turn their heads as quickly as a dog going after a flea on its back if they see anyone trying to sneak a photo for nothing.

"How long has this been going on?" I asked.

"Long enough to make the old man rich," I was told. "On a good day he takes in maybe 100 Hong Kong dollars, that's almost 20 dollars, U.S. They say he's put three sons through college in England. Not bad at 18 cents a picture!"

CHAPTER 19

Following the Tiny Bubbles to Nippon

WHENEVER I'M NEAR Epernay, that pretty little French town that lies at the heart of the Champagne district, I usually stop to see my friend Joe Dargent and to find out what's new in the grape squeezing business. Monsieur Dargent, to give him the dignity he deserves, is not only the head man in an organization called *Le Comité Interprofessionnel du Vin de Champagne,* a sort of trade association of all the great champagne makers, but he also happens to be the mayor of his village in the suburbs of Epernay. He is a gentle man, bearing a resemblance to Charles de Gaulle, unfailingly polite, almost never perturbed.

When I visited him one day more than a year ago, however, he was plainly upset. In answer to my irreverent question, "What's with champagne, Joe? Any new flavors?" he rose, almost sputtering, from his desk, reaching for one bottle among many others on top of a bookcase.

"What's new?" he roared, "I'll tell you what's new! Look at this! The most unthinkable thing in all my years has happened!"

Holding the offending bottle so I could see the label, he announced: "The *Japanese* are now making champagne!"

May the bones of the good monk, Dom Perignon, stir in his tomb at Hautvillers! There it was, a label all written in French, bearing the name "champagne" but also the unthinkable words: MADE AND BOTTLED IN JAPAN.

"Is the stuff any good?" I asked.

Monsieur Dargent drew himself up with deGaullean dignity. "I have no idea whether it is *good* or not," he said, "but this much I can tell you without hesitation. It is *not* champagne!"

Indeed, such has always been the attitude of the French toward immitations of their illustrious bubbly wine. And perhaps quite properly. The real stuff is named for the district north of Paris where the right combination of grapes, climate, limestone soil and great old firms like Mumm, Bollinger, and Laurent-Perrier have made champagne wine world famous. Others may fool around with fermenting sparkling wines, say the French, but there is only one champagne, monsieur, and it comes only from Champagne.

Nevertheless, the next time I traveled to Japan, I determined to try some of the Nipponese bubbly and, better yet, see it made. After all, despite a reflex puckering of the lips among wine drinkers at the mere mention of Japan, I was sure that a country that produces cultured pearls, bean curd, bullet trains, Wankel engines, Kobe beef, origami elephants and soy sauce, can surely master the technology necessary to turn grape juice into something palatable. I asked my friend Shinsaku Sogo for help.

"Where are the vineyards in Japan?" I wanted to know. "Who is making champagne? Is it possible to visit a winery the way people do in France and the U.S?"

Sogo is a businessman. He is not personally into wine, but he has connections among the zaibatsu. "I'll see what I can arrange," he said. Later that night, a message from Sogo turned up in my hotel key box. It said, "Minegishi, Director of Mann's Wine, will take you to Katsunuma tomorrow. Meet him at seats 22–24, 9 A.M. Limited Express, Asakusa railroad station."

I felt like a spy. How would I know Minegishi? How would he know me? What was Katsunuma? And what was Mann's Wine? A picture of Joe Dargent holding that bottle aloft returned. I was on my way into enemy territory. Would I ever be welcomed back in Epernay?

The next morning the rendezvous went easily. There was Minegishi, sitting in his reserved seat, waiting for me to take the one next to him. He was a man past fifty, dark suit, white shirt, dark tie, thinning hair, with an easy smile. He seemed a little shy. He wasn't quite clear why this person from New York wanted to see his winery but he was making a trip to Katsunuma today anyway, so I was welcome to come along.

We talked as the train headed for Yamanashi Prefecture, which is called the fruit bowl of Japan because most of the country's grapes, plums and peaches come from there. A mountainous area, it lies west of Tokyo and just north of the great cone of Mt. Fuji. It would take over an hour to get to the town of Katsunuma, Mr. Minegishi said; was there anything in particular I wanted to know about before we got there?

I decided to start with the sore point about champagne. That way, I thought, our relationship could only get better if my first questions offended him.

"I have a good friend in France who is very upset because you Japanese are making champagne," I said.

Minegishi kept his poise. "Yes, I know," he said, quite seriously, "and because of the French objections, we are going to stop."

"Stop making champagne?"

"No, we are going to stop calling it champagne," he said with a laugh. "You Americans are the only country in the world who can get away with that name, apparently. We will switch to the general term, 'sparkling wine'. When I went to France, they were very insistent about this." Did he meet a man named Dargent?

"That could have been his name," said Minegishi. "A tall man with a moustache? In Epernay?"

"Yes," I said, "that's him."

"Of course, we make other wines besides champagne," Minegishi said. "We make reds, whites, a rosé and a brandy. We Japanese have been making wine from grapes for over a hundred years. It's nothing new for us. The grapes came here over 800 years ago from China."

What is new in Japan is an American-style boom in wine consumption: 6 million domestic bottles in 1971, 9 million in 1972, 18 million in 1973 and still going up. Minegishi said his company expected to increase its wine output by 50 percent a year for the next 10 years.

Imported wines are booming too. In 1973 a French Chateaux Margaux went on sale for $30 a bottle at the Mitsukoshi department store in Tokyo and to quote a Japanese newspaper sold "like hot cakes" as a gift item. Other French wines sell briskly at $8 to $12 a bottle. Even at such prices, the Japanese still drink more imported wine than domestic varieties, though the latter average under $2 per bottle.

I asked if it were mostly young people whose drinking habits were changing.

"Not just young people, but it seems everybody up to 50," was the answer. "It is partly because many Japanese have traveled and seen other people all over the world enjoying wine. Also because our own diet is changing and we are eating more protein-rich foods that go well with table wines."

But wine is still a small fraction of Japan's alcoholic intake, my host explained. In 1973 the average Japanese consumed 33 litres (about 8 gallons) of beer, 16 litres of sake (distilled rice wine), 2 litres of grain alcohol, 1½ litres of whiskey and 1½ litres of everything else—including wine.

The train moved along through rural foothill country, stopping at small towns where houses had red tile roofs. Takao. Otsuki. Orchards grew on the hillsides, occasionally vineyards. The vines seemed to spread about five feet off the ground on overhead wire trellises strung between poles. Minegishi pointed to the small farms and said that despite heavy demand and good prices, it was very difficult to get Japanese farmers interested in growing grapes. He explained that there was a government subsidy of $1700 per hectare (2½ acres) per year for farmers who will switch from rice (on which yields per hectare are now high) to grapes. But there have been few takers.

"The farmers remember that government agricultural policies haven't always worked out so well in the past," Minegishi said with a wry smile. "First it was sugar cane that Tokyo encouraged. That flopped. Then it was hops for beer. But you could buy them cheaper in Europe, so that failed. Now the farmers think grapes may be just another cockeyed scheme."

So there is both a wine boom and a grape shortage in Japan. The result is that Japanese vintners are buying vineyards in the U.S. and even in the Bordeaux region of France. They are also importing more than 4 million litres of foreign wines in bulk from France, West Germany, Italy, Algeria and Chile every year. Meantime, such is the need for greater production at home that the leading companies send agricultural technicians out into farm areas to explain viticulture—and to offer farmers contracts which guarantee purchase of their crops for 15 years.

♦ ♦ ♦

Katsunuma is a small town with a quiet railroad station and a couple of taxis. Minegishi hailed one of these, had a conference with the driver, then beckoned me to come along. "I want to show you our experimental vineyards first," he said. "They are 700 meters high up in the hills. We couldn't find any land lower down."

The reason was plain enough when we started up a rutted, tire-bursting road in the Datsun cab. Every small plot of land was planted with fruit trees, grape vines, mulberry bushes, persimmons. Close up, I could see that the grape arbors were indeed high enough to walk under and that the thick overhead canopy of vines all grew from only a few plants. Minegishi said that with Koshu grapes, the most common Japanese variety, 150 plants per hectare is enough. In the U.S. the average is 3000 plants in the same area.

Up the mountain we went, lurching and growling in low gear until we came to a large cultivated area of young vines, some of them hardly big enough to reach the wire trellis. There was fog in the valleys at this altitude, but when it lifted occasionally, we could see the outline of Fujiyama in the near distance.

"This is our test area," my guide said. "Mann's *nojo*. That means farm. We are growing 100 varieties of grapes from all over the world here to see which will be best. There is good light and sun on this south side of the hill, there is the good influence of Mt. Fuji—and there is something else that is important. I will show you."

We let the cab go at this point and walked along a tractor road between the vines until we came to a small spring at the edge of some woodland. A stone monument had been erected next to the source of bubbling water. It was inscribed with Japanese characters.

"This is an old—what we call *Waka* poem," Minegishi said with what seemed a slightly embarrassed pride. "The words say, 'Thanks to this endless water flow, the little grapes of this mountain taste good.' That's not just right in English, but in Japanese it is poetic." He bowed slightly toward the spring.

There is a company experimental station located on the *nojo* and we walked there to talk with Mitsuo Tasaki who is in charge of the farm. He was a pleasant man in his forties who wore a gray company uniform, complete with cap. He had studied agriculture and viticulture at the University of Chiba. His greatest accomplishment to date is the development of a seedless variety of the Delaware grape—which he says happened by accident when he was experimenting with a new hormone to produce bigger bunches. I asked him which of the 100 varieties growing under Mt. Fuji's benign influence looked like the grapes of the future for Japan.

"It is not yet possible to say," he replied, "but we are having good results with both Cabernet Sauvignon and Gros Sèmillon. But we believe that the results are not entirely up to us. The grapes themselves will decide what is the best land to grow in. If they grow, they grow." It sounded like the philosophy of another Waka poem.

Tasaki then added, however, that some things could be controlled, that the company was studying the economics of vine cultivation and had, with new methods and mechanization, reduced man hours per hectare from 4000 per year to 1000. He said the figure is 700 man hours per year in Europe and 250 in the U.S.

"We are catching up with you," he commented quite seriously.

We talked about grapes while sampling several varieties which Tasaki washed and presented to us, along with oshibori towels. He said he thought Japan might eventually have better success with white wines and German varieties of grapes. "Our weather is more like Germany," he explained, "and Japanese people seem to like white wines better than red anyway. Perhaps it is because of the fish we eat—or the conditioning of sake."

Then we went down the mountain in a company car to the winery for a tasting.

"People say our plant looks like a petroleum refinery," Minegishi said, laughing apologetically. He was right. It is a small cluster of one-story warehouse-like buildings with metal roofs and a "tank farm" capable of storing a million litres of wine in huge glass-lined containers. There is the usual industrial confusion of pressing machinery (French), hoses, filters, pumps and stainless steel tanks in the production areas and a single small cellar where some limited quantities of wine are stored in casks of imported Limousin (French) oak. There was also a small copper brandy still made by Alambic of Cognac (France).

A few truckloads of grapes were coming into the plant, although the harvest in the Katsunuma region was by now almost finished. Truckloads of big, reddish Koshus were arriving, packed in 18-pound Australian cheese boxes because there just weren't enough of the usual plastic baskets.

After a look around, we were invited to a reception room where several other members of the company seemed pleased to take an afternoon break and greet a visitor from America. I signed the guest book. A conference table was set with bottles of wine, glasses, a basket of dry (French) bread and a large ceremonial candle that looked like it came from a Bavarian gift shop. There were plaques and awards on the walls: a Grand Prix from Budapest in 1966, a Monde Selection from Paris, 1967.

Soon corks were drawn and sniffed and various wines were splashed into tulip glasses: a one-year-old vin rosé, "vintage" Sèmillon and Cabernet, white Koshu, a medium-priced red and white wine called simply "Gold," an inexpensive white named Silvia—and Mann's champagne, "demi sec."

As we sipped and talked and held various wines on our tongue, I noted that all the labels were marked, *"Premier Grand Cru. Mis en bouteille dan nos caves."* Not having seen any *caves* to speak of, I asked why a Japanese company felt the need to use French terms to describe their products, even those made from Chinese grapes.

"We are going to stop that!" said Dr. Katsuyasu Ueno, another company director. He was good natured but emphatic. "You see, in the beginning, we were trying to make French-type wines, but now we are shifting to Japanese styles which are better. It is the same in sports in Japan. At first, we played baseball with the same ball you use in the U.S. Now we use our own ball which is altogether different and an improvement. Even a Japanese tennis ball is not the same. It is softer. We start out adopting other people's style, but then we always improve on it."

I asked about the champagne again.

"Yes," said Ueno, twirling a glass of Mann's own two-year-old bubbly by the stem. "But our champagne is not really the French type anyway. We use the German method of two fermentations, both in vats. This eliminates the need to disgorge the sediment after a length of time and re-cork the bottle. Much more efficient."

Japanese champagne, I learned as more was poured into my glass, is blended at the second fermentation stage, but no sugar or liqueur is added. It is aged one year in tanks, one year in the bottle and is then sent to market. Cost about $3 a bottle.

"After the third year," Ueno said, "the taste declines. We don't know why."

More wine arrived. The tasting turned into an impromptu party with each celebrant appropriating a bottle of his choice for steady drinking. The bread was gone. The Bavarian candle burned lower. The room was getting warm. Some of the wine began to taste quite good to a non-discriminating palate. But I needed more bread to be sure. I also needed some fresh air.

Soon Ueno announced, "I think I can tell you now that our company is going to have its own chateau!" Others around the table smiled broadly and looked at me, obviously pleased that the boss had decided to reveal this grand plan to the guest.

"We are doing this because we have seen that almost all companies in this business have a chateau of their own," Ueno went on. "It is a very big ambition for us and will take five years to complete."

I was afraid to ask. "Will the architecture of the chateau be French?"

"No, no," said Ueno. "Not western style. That would not be appropriate. It will be a Japanese chateau."

The bottles kept coming and other facts about the company kept emerging. Mann's Wine, presently No. 2 in its field (Mercian is No. 1, Suntory No. 3) is a 12-year-old division of the Kikkoman Group, best known for the soy sauce it has been brewing since 1661. And did I know, Minegishi asked, that in Japan the average per capita consumption of soy sauce, man, woman and child, is 10 litres per year, while the consumption of wine is .09 litres per year? Of course, I didn't. Somehow, it seemed an inverted sense of taste.

Then, as the tasting-turned-party rolled on, corporate pride prompted another announcement. "Because we work on all aspects of cultivation, you might be interested to know that we have developed a new device for use in the vineyards which will reduce the losses of grapes to birds!" I couldn't imagine what would come next.

"In cooperation with a leading Japanese transistor firm, we now have an electronic scarecrow which has been scientifically designed to keep almost all types of birds away from the vines."

The time had come to sink slowly into the sunset. I made departure movements.

"But you haven't told us which wine you like best," Ueno protested pleasantly. "You can't leave without telling us." I was trapped. I didn't really want to say anything. I'm a poor judge.

"That low-priced Silvia was good," I said lamely but truthfully.

"Isn't that interesting!" Ueno and the other said almost in a chorus, looking at each other. "When the French ambassador was asked about our products he said, 'With Japanese wines, the cheaper they are, the better they are.' "

I felt somewhat relieved at that. It's always nice to have a Frenchman's opinion of wine on your side.

I took one more sip of the champagne. It was too warm to judge by now, but I wanted to try and remember that taste. I knew Joe Dargent would ask me about it the next time I was in Epernay.

CHAPTER 20

Hong Kong—At Your Service

THE AMERICAN businessman had just arrived in Hong Kong and after a long wait around the claim area, it became obvious that his bags were lost. Anxious inquiries produced nothing but apologies from the airline involved. The luggage would surely turn up, they said, perhaps tomorrow. . . . In the meantime, there was nothing to do but go on to the hotel. The man passed through customs with just his briefcase in hand and went to find the airport representative of the Mandarin Hotel where he had reservations.

"Your bags, sir?" said the efficient young Chinese who wore the distinctive Mandarin "M" on his uniform.

"Lost," muttered the American, waving despondently.

"Excuse me, sir," said the man from Mandarin. "I will make a call . . ."

Twenty minutes later, after a quick non-stop ride through the new tunnel under Hong Kong's teeming harbor, the business-man was greeted at the Mandarin's reception desk by a tall, dignified concierge in a frock coat.

"We're terribly sorry about your luggage," said D.W. Nickols, "but you'll find what we call our 'survival kit' in your room. It should help you manage until the bags show up."

And, indeed, there it was on the bed—shirts, underwear, socks, a crisp handkerchief, an electric razor, toothbrush, toothpaste . . .

"A really marvelous service," said the American later, "and everything fit! How did you know my sizes?"

"Our man at the airport phoned them in," explained Mr. Nickols as if nothing could be more logical after all.

An apocryphal tale? No, true. An extraordinary sort of stunt to get publicity? Not in Hong Kong, where some of the world's greatest hotels render some of the world's most exceptional services to their guests and consider it routine.

I've been going to Hong Kong off and on ever since 1963 when the Colony had just over 200,000 annual tourists and the elegant old Peninsula was the undisputed *grande dame* among the hotels. Today, the "Pen" is still old, elegant and *grande*, but there are more than 40 other hotels, some of them elegant, many of them new and all of them in fierce competition to rent a total of 11,000 guest rooms. By the end of 1976, the number of rooms will increase to almost 20,000 as two million people a year are expected to visit the glittering bazaar by the China Sea.

Obviously, if Hong Kong hotels are famous for seeking a competitive edge on their rivals, they will soon be more so. In the meantime, it would be hard to find a keener game of hotel one-upmanship than is going on right now in the shadow of Victoria Peak.

As in the case of the American businessman, tender loving care of guests often begins at the airport. Most hotels have staff members on hand to greet arriving guests. The Excelsior attaches enough importance to this service to assign an assistant manager to airport duty.

It also goes without saying that all hotels are prepared to pick guests up in private or hired cars—a custom instituted long ago, incidentally, to protect the *hotel* from having its guests lured away to some other hostelry at the last minute by airport touts. The real gamesmanship began, however, when the Peninsula decided that *its* guests should be transported in nothing less than Rolls-Royces and thereupon bought a fleet of seven Silver Ghosts for the purpose. (They are also available for rental to guests for $14 per hour.)

The Mandarin, one of the Pen's principal cross-harbor rivals for the title of Number One in Hong Kong, promptly responded with its own Rolls service. The Hilton opted for Mercedes-Benz limousines, followed by the Excelsior (Hong Kong's largest hotel with 1003 rooms) which has just purchased a fleet of 20 air-conditioned Mercedes.

For all its four million people (99 percent Chinese) Hong Kong is a small town and rumors fly quickly. When Peninsula announced that it would trade its 7 Rolls for 8 Lincoln Continental limousines, a chauvinist shock passed right through Government House. Now *they say* the Furama hotel has located a rare old Bugatti at an incredible price . . .

Competitors' press releases notwithstanding, the Hilton insists that *it* began the custom of greeting an incoming guest with a cup of jasmine tea served in the room only minutes after arrival. Like many other elegant touches, this one proved popular with guests and contagious with other hotel keepers. Some boast that the tea gets to the room before the guest's bags, other say they use an exclusive China service patterned after authentic antiques. Of course, once a thing like this gets going, someone has to be different. The Mandarin sniffed and decided to ignore the whole business of tea.

As in Singapore and other Asian cities, there was for some time a rivalry among Hong Kong hotels to see who could have the biggest and most elegant Sikh as a doorman. The tall, turbanned men of this Indian sect are swarthy and arrogant chaps who revel in outrageously decorative uniforms—and in the tips that flow like a river of easy gold to the doorman at any leading hotel. The Sikh game turned sick, however, when one of the leading establishments found to its dismay that its very own 6-foot ornament was shaking down cabdrivers for the right to pick up fares at *his* front door.

The Peninsula kept aloof from this mini-scandal because it had remained steadfastly committed to an endearing front-door crew of little Chinese boys in crisp, white uniforms, pillbox hats and black mandarin slippers. In fact, a form of reverse snobism applied: the *smaller* the boys, the cuter the guests thought they were. The law requires that they be at least 14; some look 10 —and rake in tips accordingly.

One of the Hilton's exclusive competitive weapons for many years has been ownership of a 110-foot brigantine called the *Wan Fu* which cruises Hong Kong harbor with patrician grace and takes groups of guests on two scheduled cruises daily. A two-masted replica of the old Royal Navy pirate chasers of the last century, *Wan Fu* also makes special cruises at the time of Chinese festivals—and, of course, because this is Hong Kong, where the guest is king, *Wan Fu* can be booked for private parties, complete with captain and crew. No other Hong Kong hotel has its own boat and, curiously, none seems anxious to challenge *Wan Fu*.

All leading Hong Kong hotels are engaged in the continuous, not periodic, process of room refurbishing and redecorating with the result that there are not only some gaudily elegant suites available, but many standard rooms with dramatic decorator touches. At the Mandarin, a low-key richness prevails: brushed pewter bathroom hardware, Italian tile, hand caned door panels, massive brass lamps, rich drapes and soft carpeting create the mood—but if the furniture doesn't happen to suit a particular guest's needs, the Mandarin stands ready to change every stick of it to suit. Another lamp, sir? Of course. A different chair? A larger desk? Double beds merged into kingsize? A movie projector? Right away. The Mandarin displays an unblinking calm in the face of almost any request. If the 16 generously proportioned, Swedish-made teakwood coathangers supplied in each closet are not sufficient, more will arrive within the minute. Only the 700 individual coil springs in each custom-made Mandarin box spring mattress are a number which the guest is expected to accept as being beyond the possibility of change.

A first-time visitor at the Peninsula is asked to make a critical decision shortly after arrival in his room. "Roomboy," that venerable tradition of all the best Hong Kong hotels, will present an assortment of nine of the world's best known soaps and inquire which the guest prefers. The choice, once made, is not only reflected henceforth in the bathroom, but also becomes a matter of the guest's permanent record. Since 40 percent of the Pen's business comes from old friends returning, they need never again have to specify their favorite soap. Likewise, if the Pen's head bartender remembers that a returning guest's favorite cocktail is, say, a Sazerac, the drink may arrive at his table first night without being ordered.

It's all part of the trick of making people feel at home, says the Peninsula. That's why they quietly make a note of the date-of-birth on guests' passports—and send them unexpected birthday cards all over the world.

Hotel dining rooms are, inevitably, prime competitive battle-grounds and it would be impossible to overestimate the importance of cuisine and its presentation.

For a guest's party of 24, the Mandarin once prepared a replica of a Ch'ing Dynasty imperial banquet which took three months to research and three days to serve. It featured such exotic items as bear paws, crane legs and rice bird tongues. But even for its "ordinary" day-to-day menus, the Mandarin imports Dutch veal, Swedish pork and New Zealand lamb; smoked salmon from Hokkaido, rock oysters from Sydney, grouse from Scotland; and strawberries from around the world in season.

The Plaza, Hong Kong's newest hotel, is an 850 room beauty operated by Japan Air Lines in the newly developing Causeway Bay area. Anxious to enhance its appeal to American tourists, the Plaza will feature a San Francisco Steakhouse Restaurant complete with cable car and U.S. beef.

At the Hilton, luncheon buffets presented each day in the Golden Lotus and the Den are the most spectacular in town, complete with ice carvings, margarine sculptures and enough food for a Roman banquet in a DeMille movie.

Not every culinary effort involves showmanship on such a vast scale, however. One of the best deserts in town is simply a little peak-roofed, dark chocolate house served with ice cream at the Swiss-menu Chesa restaurant at the Pen. It is a trade-mark dish which tourists are often advised not to miss. Incidentally, many of the leading chefs in Hong Kong (Hilton, Hyatt, Furama, Mandarin, Peninsula, etc.) are not Chinese but Swiss.

Entertainment while dining is another opportunity for managements to come up with creative flourishes. For many years, one of the most colorful supper shows in Hong Kong has been the all-girl Chinese opera troupe which puts on two performances a night to sold-out audiences at the Miramar Hotel. This is such an extravagant and well-staged show with brilliant lighting effects, an aerial tramway and traditional Chinese music that it has proved a tough act for others to follow—i.e., imitate. For one thing, the Miramar has a corner on some of the best young performers in town.

Another exclusive group that would be hard to duplicate is the nine-piece Classical Orchestra which plays for dinner each night in the Hilton's Golden Lotus Room. Led by Lu Pei Yuen of the Hong Kong Academy of Music, the group uses traditional instruments from old China, such as the pipa, a 4-stringed tenor guitar, the cheng, a Chinese harpsichord and the erh-hwa, a two-stringed violin. Hilton says there's little danger that any other hotel can come along and match this act because there just aren't any more musicians around who can play the ancient instruments.

The Hilton adds an extra promotional touch to the evening by supplying guests with copies of Ch'ing dynasty noble's robes to wear during dinner and for souvenir photos. It all adds up to a very authentic Chinese atmosphere to go along with a classical Chinese menu.

No mention of Hong Kong's hotly competitive hotel services would be complete without an appreciation of that unique institution, the roomboy. First-time guests may not realize that the young Chinese who will knock on the room door only moments after their arrival is not a bellhop looking for a quick tip already, but more like a personal valet whose greatest pleasure is to see that *his* guests are well looked after. At the Mandarin, there are two boys permanently assigned to each floor of 32 rooms. Returning guests often request to be put in the same room so they can again have their same "boy." He will not only attend to such routine daily requirements as laundry, shoe shines, bed making and other housekeeping chores, but he will also know when you got up this morning, whether you're going sightseeing this afternoon, and what you want done with all those parcels and bags you just brought home from a shopping expedition.

If he's well trained, he'll watch your room like a guardian, knowing when you are in or out, drawing drapes against the sun, adjusting air conditioning to your taste—and always, but always, replacing bathroom towels as fast as you may use them throughout the day.

If you can't sleep, call roomboy. He may suggest hot Ovaltine —and fix it for you. If you can't stay awake but need an afternoon nap, call roomboy. He won't let you oversleep. If you want to get the kids out of your hair for a few hours, call roomboy. He knows where there's a babysitter in the hotel. Spot on your tie? Wrinkle in your lapel? Call roomboy. He'll make quick repairs. Want your picture taken on the balcony? Call roomboy. He knows how to focus a Pentax.

Roomboys, for all their unique capabilities, are not expected to supply all the services and information which a Hong Kong hotel guest might require. For more complex problems, the hotel concierge is often a fount of knowledge, particularly if he is the Mandarin's D.W. Nickols, a towering and unflappable gentleman with 32 years experience in finding ways to do the impossible.

Problem: Guest has broken upper plate, desperate to have teeth fixed as soon as possible.

Nickols: "It can be done in about an hour. This is Hong Kong."

Problem: Guest's fabric bag ripped asunder by the airline.

Nickols: "Routine. We have a man who fixes a dozen to 15 bags a day for us."

Problem: Guest has just purchased a suite of carved rosewood furniture and wants to ship it to Texas.

Nickols: "Our parcel room will take care of it."

Problem: Guest in the diamond business wants to ship some very valuable small packets.

Nickols: "The parcel room can do anything."

Problem: Single male guest is lonely. Wishes respectable female companionship for the evening.

Nickols: "We have an escort service we recommend."

Problem: Where can one get the New York closing price on IBM?

Nickols: "You'll find quotations posted daily in the Chinnery Bar."

Problem: There's a lady guest in 1516 who says she's been looking out her window at Red China for several days now and wants to know how to get there.

Nickols: "Tell her that's the Kowloon side of Hong Kong she's looking at and she can take the Star Ferry over there every three minutes."

◆ ◆ ◆

At the Excelsior, a lobby information desk manned 13 hours a day by a representative of the super-efficient Hong Kong Tourist Association is an effective and unique arrangement for handling guests' questions about shopping, sightseeing, or even "Where can I play a game of squash?" No problem, says the Excelsior, anything for a guest.

At the Peninsula in recent years, guests have been routinely referred to acupuncture practitioners on request and one regular visitor's standing order for a supply of Cuban cigars is promptly filled whenever he arrives. No problem, says the Peninsula, we're much more than a hotel.

At the new Plaza, an exclusive duty free shop in the hotel

enables guests to buy liquor, tobacco, perfume and other taxed items as they would in the airport itself. Purchases are delivered to the plane when the guest departs Hong Kong. No problem says Japan Air Lines, anything for a passenger.

Around the back side of Hong Kong island, 20 minutes from Victoria's central district and facing the China Sea, there is a lovely old 1920s hotel called the Repulse Bay which in a stucco-quaint and nostalgic way seems to epitomize all the personal attentions that the Colony's hostelries are famous for. Although its reputation is by now well assured and its 30 ocean-view suites are almost always fully booked, the hotel still maintains standards of service that even the newest and slickest would find hard to match. It has an extravagantly large staff of 200.

Repulse Bay is a serene sort of retreat that evokes the mood of another era unmarred by the pollution of today's realties. A Bentley breathes silently up to the front portico under an arch of ancient, brilliant flame trees while, beyond, an old fishing junk with patched sails seems barely moving between the islands.

"My favorite time is evening," Manager Benno Welschen told me once when we were having lunch on the hotel verandah. "You can sit here and watch the sun set across the sea and the islands look like pieces of stage scenery disappearing to the horizon."

Fresh flowers, grown in the hotel's own gardens ("only 70 days from seed—and the seeds come from England") were on every table. It was nearly 3 P.M. when a Grand Marnier soufflé was presented with quivering perfection for dessert. Time seemed not to matter at all. The junk still had not moved. Somerset Maugham would come up the steps at any moment.

"This is one of the chef's favorite dishes," Welschen explained. "Of course, he does many other special things. For example, if we happen to overhear table conversation to the effect that it is a guest's birthday, chef can usually come up with a cake and candles and the name spelled correctly on the icing in time for dessert. Compliments of the house, of course."

Of course. Because this is Hong Kong—where anything is possible.

CHAPTER 21
Business as Usual in Lebanon

THE LAST Arab–Israeli war began for me somewhere between the pickled lamb's brains and the Armenian smoked beef. I was on my way to see the great rose colored ruins at Baalbek and we had stopped at a restaurant on the road to Damascus for one of those incredible Lebanese smorgasbords called mezzeh. Mezzeh is something they talk a lot about in Beirut but seldom eat. It may have been invented just to impress tourists. At any rate, it is an impressive production: 40 or 50 small, oval dishes of assorted hors d'oeuvres: frogs legs, cheeses, peanuts, hommos, lamb tartare, pistachio nuts, baked beans, eggplant, kidneys, aromatic leaves—anything edible, "and a few things which you should *not* eat," my friend Fida warned. Fida is Lebanese. She is a schoolteacher.

The man who brought the news to our table spoke in Arabic. He was calm. There was war, he said. No, not just a border clash, but war with planes and tanks and all the other apparatus again. There was heavy fighting in Syria, he added. Syria, Fida observed, was just down the road from Baalbek.

206

"Should we turn back?" I asked.

"Oh, no. You shouldn't miss Baalbek!" The Lebanese have learned detachment. "The last war lasted only six days," Fida said. "This one may be over in three. I hope so. War is very bad for business."

Baalbek was beautiful in the setting sun. Three great temples, thousands of years old, built on foundation stones so massive that no one yet knows how they were cut or moved. One block, still lying in the quarry, is calculated to weight 1400 tons. As I pondered this piece of man's unfinished business, evening prayer sounded mournfully from a mosque nearby. Then, out of the eastern sky, came the fierce sound of a jet, a thunderclap of 20th Century anger over the Temple of Jupiter, 53 A.D.. How far away was this war? Thousands of years? A few miles?

Near Zahle, on the road back to Beirut, there was a crowd. "They are journalists," Fida explained after talking with one of them. "A war plane has fallen nearby. They are sitting around this restaurant, drinking *arraq* and waiting to see it. But if it is an Israeli plane, I could tell them: they'll find nothing because the Israelis always come in the night and pick up everything. Oh, they do everything so perfectly!"

We drove on, up through the mountains where there was mist and fog. Soldiers from an armored vehicle stopped the car once and probed the interior with the beams of their flashlights. They were young and they smiled when Fida said we were tourists. How close can a war be, I thought, when soldiers still smile?

The next morning, outside the hotel, a newsboy no more than ten was toting an armful of papers and chanting some words over and over. I couldn't read the Arabic headlines, but when the lad passed my car, he took a long look at my American face and stuck a small pink tongue out at me. I thought about him all the way up the coast road to Tripoli. What did his headlines say? Was hostility mounting?

"You keep forgetting," Fida said, "this is Lebanon. There is never anything to worry about here. It's the Switzerland of the Middle East."

We stopped at Batroun, famous for its lemons and lemonade. Fida said I should try some *kenefe begebne,* a sweet breakfast roll made with unleavened bread, cheese, sesame seeds and syrup. It tasted good with the lemonade. The shopkeeper had a radio and we asked for news of the war. He looked at me and shrugged. "He says there is no news," Fida said, but I was sure I heard the name Kissinger several times.

Tripoli is Lebanon's second city, a sunbaked sprawl of cement houses by the sea with an old Crusader castle looking down. In the castle they have found the graves of Frenchmen from Toulouse who died for Christianity in 1101. There are bones in the small stone coffins along with some empty Marlboro packs.

A few Lebanese soldiers manned a shaded guard post inside the castle's ancient gate. Their automatic rifles were propped casually against sandbags. In a wild fantasy, I imagined picking one up; the soldiers weren't watching me, they were trying to listen to war news on a transistor radio. A young man pounding Arabic designs into a large brass tray made it difficult to hear. The soldiers told him to be quiet, but he ignored them. To a Lebanese brass worker, the tourist dollar comes way ahead of any war.

In the *souk* at Tripoli I saw a French language newspaper with the headline *C'est la Guerre* and stories about fighting near the Suez, but people were paying more attention to shopping for tonight's dinner: lamb, fish, eggplant, carrots, grapes, dates. They hardly noticed a doubleknitted American visitor—but one shopkeeper did try to arouse my interest in a rug.

We went back to Beirut by way of the yacht club where there were more fancy boats than in Larchmont and you could order a very respectable hamburger with a Pepsi and watch a sunset sailboat race. There wasn't a newspaper in sight here, but pretty girls in bikinis decorated the afterdecks of some of the bigger ocean cruisers, closely watched by rich looking young men wearing gold medals on chains which nested in dark chest hair. Around the bar the talk was French, English and Arabic, but it wasn't about the war.

"Where will you be sightseeing tomorrow?" I was asked and I said I hoped to see Tyre. "That's pretty close to Israel," my friend said, as if cautioning a traveler that the roads might be congested—with tanks. "Why don't you wait a day or so until this is all over . . ."

I had to admit, in the first 24 hours of Holy War, Lebanon seemed a determinedly calm eye in a gathering storm. But I was still apprehensive. Weren't the Lebanese Arabs? And weren't all Arabs the 'other side?' Not many Americans invest in Lebanese war bonds, after all, or even know a Lebanese, other than Danny Thomas. Maybe it would be better not to stay, or come again some other time.

"Nonsense!" said Pepe Abed who is half Lebanese and half Mexican and runs a picturesque seaside restaurant in the shadow of an old Crusader castle in Biblos. "You're afraid we are *Arabs?* Don't you realize that every Lebanese is a businessman first? You don't see any war in Biblos, do you? Of course not. Pepe would not have it! It would ruin my dinner business!"

Pepe wears a yachting cap when he thinks someone is going to take his picture. He is a rakishly handsome man in his sixties who still scubas for Phoenician antiquities, supervises a

good kitchen, runs a small tour business and a smaller hotel
in Beirut and a beach club up the coast. Under a Mediterranean moon, with the fishing boats bumping each other
gently in the tight little harbor below, his Hacienda de Pepe
could be a hideaway in Baja California. The war seemed as far
away as the Romans who built the amphitheatre at Biblos
where I had watched the sun set. Pepe and his place were
good for the nerves.

"Wartime" Beirut was part Oriental bazaar, part European
resort. Its streets swarm with old yellow Mercedes taxis that
have eyes painted on their radiators and colored lights shining
behind their beat-up grilles at night. They cruise near the hotels
and shops, rolling up quietly behind pedestrians with a toot of
the horn and a smiling solicitation from the driver. "American,
you are welcome," one says. "Hello New York," says another.
Shopkeepers stand in doorways like ladies of the night, apprais-
ing each passer-by, murmuring invitations, twirling amber
worry beads with the skill of compulsive yo-yo champions.
Somewhere in this city on the second day of Holy War, Pales-
tinians were mapping strategies against Israeli settlements and
the government maintained a tip-toe neutrality, but in the
streets it was business as usual.

There are dozens of hotels in Beirut, but two command all
the attention: the fashionable St. George and, across the street,
the American-style Intercontinental-Phoenicia, complete with
pool, coffee shop, pancakes with syrup and a waiter wandering
around the lobby dressed like the Arabian Nights and carrying
a pot of Arabian coffee for anyone who wants a jigger of the
sticky stuff. He keeps repeating, "You are welcome, you are
welcome," in a sort of chant.

The St. George is the place to have important luncheons by
the sea; the Phoenicia is the place to watch a somewhat laun-

dered belly dance in the supper club. As the Egyptian armies enlarged their bridgeheads on the east bank of the Suez, a woman's group held a fashion show at the St. George and airline crews continued to fill the lobby of the Phoenicia with gold braid and overnight bags. The concierge assured all who asked that even if *some* airlines were cancelling their service in and out of Beirut, there would be no question that Middle East Airlines would continue to fly.

"MEA flies when the others won't because no Lebanese is ever too afraid to make money," he said and guests chuckled at his little ethnic joke. A war without warfare can be exciting for all.

The president of Lebanon has a summer residence in the cool mountains, 30 miles from Beirut. It is a pleasant drive up to an altitude of 2600 feet; the country could be Italy or parts of Greece. The princely 19th Century palace has some elegant reception rooms, graceful balconies, many arches and fountains. There is a modest museum where you may be the only visitor on quiet days. It seemed a good place to escape into Lebanese history, to pass a day during what everyone said should be a short war. No Lebanese seems to believe in *Jihad,* the Holy War. That, they say, is for desert Arabs and crazies.

"You were at Biet Eddine today?" I was asked at dinner. "What luck! You must have seen the Israeli fighters!" Alas, I had not. "They were right there in those mountains; they shot up a Lebanese radar station." I began to wonder how long this philosophy of business-as-usual was going to survive. How cool could Arabs be? And for how long? Wouldn't tomorrow perhaps be a good day to leave Lebanon?

We went out for a final night on the town. The Fontana Club is just across from the American embassy, so the armored vehicles and sandbagged gun emplacements in the street seemed as much for the protection of the club and its guests as for His Excellency, our ambassador, whoever he is. The soldiers were leaning on the tank treads, talking and smoking as we walked by. The pop music of the Middle East drifted out of the Fontana and into the street and mixed with the crackling voices of the military walkie-talkies.

"Come in. You are welcome. You are welcome," the fat man in the tuxedo said. There were bottles of White Horse and Johnny Walker Red already on each table. Musicians with violins, a kanoun, flute, accordian, tambour, bongos and a lute sat in a row of kitchen chairs on a brightly enameled stage complete with Christmas tinsel. The girls who would dance when they got around to it were sitting out front with the customers, smoking and drinking something called K-Kola out of old Coca-Cola bottles. They were plump and very pale and laughed a lot, but when they danced it was serious seduction and Arab males made gutteral sounds of appreciation.

The Israeli fighters finally showed up over Beirut on the day we were leaving. From the balcony of our hotel room we watched the jets streak across the harbor like great metal birds twisting in the sun and leaving the blasting sound of their passage to come moments later. In the streets below, the yellow taxis still cruised at the same speed while soldiers ran with guns in their hands and shoved off into the harbor in commandeered speedboats. A few booms of aerial gunfire echoed between the hotels. Figures appeared on rooftops, shading their eyes, pointing. The enemy had just passed through Lebanon on his way home.

Around the Phoenicia pool, the beautiful people in Mediterranean tans and Paris bikinis didn't even look up from their paperbacks as the Phantoms cracked the sound barrier, nor did waiters pause in their rounds, delivering drinks and cheeseburgers. A maintainance man whom we had named Harry the Hose went on watering the poolside shrubs. It was a lovely, sunny afternoon in Beirut. Obviously, nobody was going to let a few Israelis in fighter planes spoil it.

CHAPTER 22
Travels in Tuscany

THE ALFA MADE a high-pitched sound in third gear as we climbed the narrow road from the valley. The driver knew his way well and steered around each curve with a stiff-arm style that would have done justice to one of the great Italian *pilotos*. When we pulled to the top of the ridge, he swung off the road on the apron of the last hairpin and stopped. The view was a painting, a classic Italian landscape.

"Look down there," Roger Lucas said. "That's the castle where we'll be staying tonight."

It stood, like a piece from a chess set, amid the rich greens of midsummer; a great round tower at one corner and four walls with lesser towers and tile roofs, all burnt umber and gray-brown in color.

"It's 12th Century, at least most of it is," Roger said. "The Antinoris added to it over the years."

In the distance, beyond the castle, there were vineyards, the orderly rows looking like ranks of soldiers marching on rolling terrain.

The Alfa blew a higher note as we went down the hill on the

road to the castle and for a moment I permitted myself to believe that this was all real, that the Renaissance was in flower, that Italy's golden age had never passed and that here, in this valley, one could live on in a sort of perpetual tranquility—no matter wars or pollution or hunger or other inhumanities.

The road grew narrower and the sturdy farm people we passed stepped back into the weeds, letting the car pass, some of them raising a hand in greeting.

"They probably know the car," Roger said. "I like to bring people here because I like to come myself. After Florence in the summer, this place is peace."

We had come from Florence this afternoon, a hundred miles across Tuscany, to the gates of Castello La Sala. The late sun washed the ancient stones in mellow light as the man wearing the apron came out from a small door to take our bags. There was friendly greeting all around and we were taken almost at once to see the new pups in the kennel while a species of fierce little game hens pecked dryly in the gravel of the courtyard and doves fluttered from the eaves of the great tower.

♦ ♦ ♦

Italy is many things to many travelers. It is a country of great variety, made more so by the fact that it is long and narrow, reaching across the Mediterranean like an unfinished bridge from Europe's snowy alps almost to Africa. It is a 700-mile core sample, its climate and characteristics bisected by a spine of mountains and subdivided by river valleys. It is now more than a century since Italy became one country politically, yet the parts that united to form the whole in 1870 have kept their individuality. Neither Fascism nor television nor millions of Fiats have succeeded in making one people of the Italians. The Neapolitan is still as different from a Genoese as he was when the Caesars ruled.

Yet, if there is a classic region of Italy, a place of romance where the land looks like we think Italy should, where the wine is the best and the language spoken is the purest and the history has the longest unbroken lines and the culture the richest traditions, then it must be this place called Tuscany—Toscana, the ancient land of the Etruscans, forebears of the Romans.

Florence, the capital of Italian culture, cradle of the Renaissance, is also the capital of Tuscany. The beautiful city of the Medicis has become, particularly in summer, the crowded city of the Americans. After Rome itself, Florence is the country's greatest tourist attraction, a city of churches and art galleries and beautiful stores and fine restaurants and slick airline offices. It straddles the Arno like a summer fair, banners flying, cameras clicking, shop windows agleam with gold, great bells tolling and, oh the smell of food that drifts from the trattorie!

Tuscany is not only the cradle of Italian civilization, but it is, says Michelin, "where Italian cooking was born, at the court of the Medici." Sabatini's and Doney's are the chic restaurants in Florence today—but for informal atmosphere, for the authentic flavor of Tuscany, a trattoria is best. At Latini, in Via dei Palchetti, very little English is spoken, there is no menu and hams hang from the ceiling, but they will make you feel at home and feed you well. Slightly less rustic (i.e., tablecloths) is Camillo's in Borgo San Jacopo where you are greeted as a friend on your second visit and the food may simply be the best in Florence.

◆ ◆ ◆

We entered the castle, stepping through a small door which was cut into a larger one, the great gate itself. The flat stone floor within was smoothed by ages of traffic. There was a small chapel just inside the gate and an inner court, a plain rectangular yard about the size of three tennis courts, surrounded on the four sides by plain two- and three-story stone buildings whose outer faces were the castle's walls. It was quiet and cool in here, now that the sun had turned red and reached only the tile roofs above. Geraniums tumbled from window boxes. Somewhere, a radio played.

"When the Antinoris restored the tower, they found human bones in a chamber at the bottom!" Lucas is a cosmopolitan young Englishman in charge of marketing Antinori wines around the world. He was running his favorite guided tour for two friends—and what castle's story, after all, would be complete without human bones?

"Come on," he said, "into the cellars with you both before you go to your room! I want you to see the wines you'll be drinking tonight."

We walked carefully down slippery stone stairs until we were far below ground level, somewhere beneath the heavy walls, 800 years of masonry piled above. In the dim light the wine barrels were festooned with furry white muffs and delicate lacework, fragile growths nourished by moisture and alcohol. The air itself seemed aged, as if trapped by the centuries. Breathing was like drinking; countless seasons of fermentation had left a tangible record.

When we were back in the courtyard, the warmth of the present made Karen shiver quickly. Italian castles were new to both of us. Now we wanted to see the rooms, to get on with the make-believe.

"Dinner soon," Roger said. "But we'll have a tasting first, so don't be long washing up."

From the tall, narrow window of our room we could see a bend in the road on which we had arrived; a boy was leading sheep down the hill. On the distant horizon, the old citadel of Orvieto made a dark shape against the evening sky.

Later Roger said, "Tomorrow we'll go to Orvieto—but that's

not Tuscany, you know." Our host was drawing corks and filling glasses and apologizing that since there would be just the three of us, we would dine in a small sitting room that the family uses rather than in the great, long banquet hall with the two-story-high timbered ceiling.

"We're actually just in a corner of Umbria here, but it's like Tuscany, the same feeling . . ."

◆   ◆   ◆

The feeling of Tuscany. Why is this place so *Italian* to the visitor's eye? Certainly Rome is Italian; it's famed ruins are national trademarks. Naples is romantic, its music crying with emotion. Milan is tailored elegance. But Tuscany is a wine bottle in its straw jacket. It is cypresses standing like dark sentinels, and eternal olive groves, silvery green leaves looking too young and fresh for the gnarled old arms and bodies from which they sprout. Somehow, I thought, you have seen all this before, haven't you? The hill towns, the terra cotta vases, the white oxen. It was as if I had already been here . . . when?

Then one day, in an art gallery in Florence, I found an answer to Tuscany's curious déjá vu. It was there in the paintings, in the work of the Renaissance masters. Although their foreground subjects were the saints and the martyrs and the holy family, their backgrounds were Tuscany. See for yourself at the Uffizi. Look behind the madonna and child. There are the pines and the low hills and the filtered light—and even the castles of Tuscany. And these things are all still there. You must go look for them, of course, because there is also our 20th Century in the form of too many automobiles, too many people, too much of too much. Alas, they'll serve you frozen food in some places in Florence today and they'll cook it in Wesson oil, perhaps, and some of the articles for sale in the Straw Market are surely not the work of Florentine craftsmen, and it's true

that the 1966 flood devastated some of the treasures that the
Nazis didn't steal 25 years earlier—but don't let anyone tell you
that it's all spoiled. Tuscany lives.

◆ ◆ ◆

"Do you remember, at the Antinori Palace," Roger was
asking, "just inside the big door, there is a small window?" We
nodded. The Antinori Palace is an imposing 14th Century landmark in the center of Florence, all stone and pure of line, with
the traditional overhanging roof. It is the ancestral home of this
family of merchant princes who were bankers and silk exporters
and, beginning in 1385, wine makers.

"They used to sell the wine to the people through that little
window."

Today there is a small Antinori-operated restaurant in the
palace which is open to the public. On hot, busy summer days
it is a cool and unhurried place to have lunch—and to sample
an extraordinary selection of wines by the glass.

In Florence you can be a Marquis and still sell. Often your
product is as distinguished as your lineage: Gucci, Schaparelli,
Pucci. Aristocrats of taste. Heirs to 30 centuries of civilization.
The Florentines, Italians will tell you, are polished people;
Romans are rude. Of course, rude old Napoleon's family came
from around here, from Tuscany. He came back to visit his
ancestral home town once. They gave him a reception. But in
Florence he was just a soldier–emperor and they still considered
him rough.

◆ ◆ ◆

How many cities and towns are there in Tuscany, how many
places to see, to know? With patience, you could count them
all on their hilltops and behind their walls and you might lay
out a motor route which would cover most of them. For example, westward from Florence, following a good road through

pretty country you could see Prato, famous for its wool, and Pistoia with its street of the goldsmiths bustling with activity, and walk on Lucca's remarkable parapets and, finally, see Pisa with its leaning tower, all trussed up now so it won't fall down.

Look at the map again: Tuscany's face is to the sea and its back is to the mountains. From Florence, a determined tourist might travel east into the hills and find cooler and cleaner air in summer. The Etruscan town of Fiesole, older than Florence, is 1000 feet higher than the Arno, yet it is only a 20-minute city bus ride from Piazza San Marco. There's a good restaurant there called Raspanti's and there are Roman ruins, including a beautifully situated ampitheatre where concerts are given on summer evenings. If you press on eastward, up a winding road through the mountains, you'll find a little jewel of a town called La Consuma, deep in the chestnut forests at 3000 feet.

Come back by way of Pontesieve, if you want to visit one of the biggest commercial wineries in the world, the Ruffino "works." The Girrarosto restaurant in Pontesieve serves a delicious chicken on the spit.

◆   ◆   ◆

At home we would have said we had Chianti with our steak. At Castel La Sala this evening, we had a little steak with the Santa Christina. Tuscany not only produces all of the world's Chianti, but also the best beef in Italy; two facts which, in themselves, recommend the area to American tastes. The beef is not the thick, blood-red Chicago variety, but neither is it veal passed off as beef.

Candles flickered ruby shafts of light through the wine and a quiet woman from the kitchen moved softly around the table, serving the evening's guests, making sure that the "weary travelers" were well fed.

"It is the same when the Antinoris are here," Roger said.

"Always very simple. This is the countryside, the farm. There's never a menu, only what is good that day."

What is also good in Tuscany are the truffles. And the oil. "The oil was always pressed and sold by the wine makers," Roger said.

◆ ◆ ◆

The charms of Tuscany's countryside notwithstanding, travelers would not come here without paying, at the very least, a few hours of tribute to the glories of Florence's churches and art galleries. In truth, for many it is all too much culture, too much history to confront in a short visit. But there are highpoints and landmarks that are memorable: Michaelangelo's arrogantly beautiful David, standing in his own sun-lit rotunda at the Academy of Fine Arts, a marble giant, loftily unaware of the adoring throngs at his feet; Ghiberti's bronze panels on the doors of the Baptistry—which Michaelangelo said could be the Gates to Paradise itself; the pathetic naked-wood remains of Cimabue's flood-ravaged crucifix, sad as a broken heart.

In a few days in Florence, the names of Giotto and Donatello may become familiar, but the Uffizi and Pitti Palace are strong medicine and may best be taken in small doses. A day devoted to the classical past deserves a day in the sunshine of the present —by the Arno, watching the fishermen catch nothing, along the shady paths of the Boboli Gardens, and at the summit of Fort Belvedere where one can watch the setting sun gild all the battlemented towers and sacred domes of the city with the embers of another day.

◆ ◆ ◆

We left the castle in the morning and drove to Orvieto, the walled town built atop a flat mountain called a *massif.* The car climbed a foothill road, then echoed through a stone arch in the walls and threaded through dark, narrow streets to the cathedral square. To many visitors, the duomo at Orvieto is more interesting than any church in Florence. There are wine cellars beneath the square too—indeed, beneath the cathedral itself—and there are wine shops where a thirsty traveler can buy a *panata* of cool, white Orvieto. The man and his wife behind the counter will explain the various types of this wine and offer tastes of one sort and another if you're interested. When you put your liras down, they smile like friends who are accepting the repayment of a small loan.

◆ ◆ ◆

From Orvieto, the road back to Florence passes through Siena, the second city of Tuscany, the Gothic town, a place curiously apart. Centuries ago, Siena and Florence were great enemies who fought great battles and the 50 miles that separated them became a series of fortified towns. Yet each of these big cities was rich in art and culture and each was part of the same Renaissance and contributed to it.

There is a horserace in Siena twice each summer. No, better call it an exhibition, a festival. No, not that either. A performance? An exercise in civic madness? Better. The event is called the Palio, which simply means that the prize is a gonfalon, or palio, bearing the image of the Virgin. Those who have an appreciation for passionate feelings, passionately expressed, say that this Palio is surely the ultimate emotional outburst in all of Italy.

For purposes of tradition, Siena divides itself into districts call *contrade* and for purposes of the race, each *contrade* enters a horse and hires a non-Sienese mercenary as a jockey. Wagering is intense and what the Sienese ingenuously call "alliances" are entered into between *contrade*. This means that for, say, 100,000 lira, our jockey agrees not to hit your jockey with his whip (otherwise allowed) during the race.

The Palio takes only three minutes to run, but weeks to prepare for. Even if one is not in the least interested in a fixed horserace, the medieval splendor with which the city stages its great event is a treat to the eye and to the camera lens.

◆ ◆ ◆

We drove the length of the Chianti axis, Siena to Florence, then, through the zone of Chianti Classico, where only the finest grapes make the finest wine. One of the old fortified towns crowned a hill in the distance.

"Monteriggioni," said Roger. "It's one of my favorites. We can have lunch there." And so the Alfa was pointed upward again, along the single road to the summit where all that could be seen were gray walls and square towers.

"There are fourteen of those towers. The place is really a castle that was so big they built a small town inside. Dante mentions it in the *Inferno.*"

We ate at Il Pozzo, a surprisingly pleasant little retreat in the middle of a dusty village that might have been in the wilderness of Mexico. The most expensive entre on the menu was $1.50. All the Chianti you would want with the meal: 67¢.

◆ ◆ ◆

It was almost evening when we swung back into the crunching gravel courtyard of the Palazzo Antinori in Florence. Home again, so to speak, in the big city; back to the sophistication of the Medicis. Piero Antinori greeted us.

"So," he said, looking cool in a light silk suit and smiling a patrician smile. "You like our Tuscany? There's something very special about it, isn't there?"

We agreed. Tuscany casts a spell.

CHAPTER 23
Guided Tours in Pharoahland

THEY SAY ALL the guides in Cairo are called Jimmy. I don't know about that, I only hired two and it's true they were both named Jimmy. I called one Big Jimmy because he was a rotund, heavy-breathing sort and I called the other Major Jimmy because he was said to be a retired army officer who had also perhaps been a professor.

Big Jimmy took us to the pyramids. He subcontracted the driving to his cousin Ahmed who was supposed to have a limousine, but it turned out to be a 1955 Chevrolet which carried with it, deep in its upholstery, the odor of many oil changes.

All the other guides knew Big Jimmy, of course, and they exchanged greetings in Arabic when we got to the pyramids concession. Camels were arranged for Karen and me. Jimmy said his brother-in-law's camels were absolutely the most reliable and he would see to it that we paid less because we were his friends from America.

The camels walked around for a while with us on them and

Jimmy's friends volunteered to stop the camels in the right place and take our picture in front of the pyramids, using my camera. They said they knew just how a Pentax works and, from much experience, I guess they did.

Pretty soon it was time to go inside one of the pyramids and see the small chamber that may or may not be a tomb. The interior regions were, apparently, another guide's territory because Big Jimmy turned us over to yet another of his friends.

We followed the new guide's flowing robes down a narrow stone passageway, heading for the center of the pyramid. Bare electric bulbs lighted the way along a route which is well worn by millions of tourists.

When we were almost to the bottom of the long, sloping passage, I saw another group of pilgrims, led by another guide, approaching us from the opposite direction. For a moment, it was a tight squeeze to let them pass. Everyone turned a little sideways as the two parties brushed by. Then, just as the other group's guide came stomach to stomach and face to face, he stopped as if he recognized me and then whispered loudly, "Do not go to the market with Jimmy! He is half-half with the shops." With that, he was gone.

It was to be expected, of course, that Big Jimmy might be half-half with the operators of the gift shops in the souk, but it was a shock to get the news from one of his friends in the basement of a pyramid!

After that, naturally, we called him Half-Half Jimmy.

Major Jimmy was another type, smoother, better educated. He took us to Sakkara one day and said he would drive the car himself to save us money because we were his friends from America. On the way, he warned that it was a very grave offense to take anything from any of the tombs or excavation sites where we were going, or even to take photographs in certain places. I assured him that I wouldn't do anything to embarrass him or get any of us into trouble with the authorities.

At the site of the Marble Sphinx, where some digging is still going on, the gatekeeper and all the other guides seemed to know Major Jimmy and they exchanged greetings in Arabic. One big fellow, wearing a striped thobe, called Major Jimmy aside right away and from the folds of his garment he took two small bundles of newspaper which he began to open with great care. Jimmy signalled us to come over and take a look.

"These fellows find little treasures all the time," Jimmy explained confidentially. "Little pharaonic trinkets that are so common that the archaelogists aren't even interested in them any more."

In the newspaper there were some pieces of bronze turned green with verdigris, a few small glasslike objects encrusted with sand, bits of pottery with markings—and a ring in the shape of a scarab beetle, the sacred talisman of ancient Egypt.

"Now *that* is something unusual," said Jimmy, slipping the ring on his little finger. The big fellow in the striped thobe was looking around cautiously while we pawed politely in the newspaper packages.

"He'll sell you these things for very little," Jimmy said. "I know this fellow. He is a friend of mine for many years. His things are authentic."

When we didn't show any particular interest in making a purchase or even in asking prices, Jimmy and his friend exchanged a few quick words.

Switching back to English, Jimmy then announced, "I'm taking that ring myself. I'm sure I'll never see another one like it for $25. Of course," he paused and added deferentially, "if you still want it . . ."

We still didn't.

Curiously, Jimmy lost the precious ring later that same afternoon. He was leaning over a deep excavation when he gave a little cry and said, "It's gone! My ring! The one I just bought has fallen into the old tomb." Then after another moment he said, "Oh, well, I suppose I can say I have given it back to the pharoahs."

♦   ♦   ♦

Several days later we saw our old friend Half-Half Jimmy hanging around the hotel lobby in Cairo. He came over to me and said, "I hear you've been out with one of my competitors." He said it pleasantly enough, as if it didn't matter, there were enough Americans for everybody.

Then he said, "I hope you didn't buy anything from that big fellow at Sakkara. His stuff is fake—and he was half-half with your guide."

CHAPTER 24
The Swiss Way

THE FIRST TIME I went to Switzerland was as a small boy with my mama. We took the overnight train from Paris and I fully expected that when I woke in the morning I would find myself in the midst of a winter wonderland. There would be, I was sure, great snow-covered mountains and alpine chalets and people going about on skis or sleighs. Alas for childish notions, it was summer and Switzerland was as green as Ireland. I was bitterly disappointed and felt cheated.

I've returned to Switzerland many times in later years and I've never felt disappointment again. Even as a non-skiing adult, I've learned that there's more to the Helvetian republic than snow and cable cars. This is no discovery of my own, of course. Switzerland has always been one of the major tourist destinations in Europe, an essential part of the Grand Tours of yesteryear and their less grand successors. Nevertheless, Switzerland is a place which first-time visitors sometimes fail to recognize as unique beyond its scenery.

Even second- or third-timers often fail to solve the special qualities of the Swiss.

For one thing, in a world where a great many things, systems and places don't seem to work as well as they once did, Switzerland still works, a fact which is reassuring, even comforting when you are there. It is a no-nonsense country in which people are not only famous for doing things punctually, but seem to expect no particular praise for doing them well.

"It is the Swiss way," Bruno Baroni, a Swiss with an Italian name, once told me years ago. I did not understand just what he meant then because I had seen only a little of his country and I thought he was probably using the term loosely. Now that I have returned to Switzerland more often, the term *The Swiss Way* has acquired a more precise meaning.

Of course, you say, there is an Italian way, a French way or even a Greek way, and that's true, I suppose, but I think those "ways" have come about as a result of ethnic imperatives rather than by any calculated design. The Swiss Way is more than fondue and folk songs. It is, to put it as simply as possible, a dedication to doing things right. Unfortunately, the zeal with which this is sometimes practiced strikes visitors as Eagle-Scoutism at its worst, but the Swiss are unperturbed by foreign critics.

There are people of many ethnic origins in Switzerland and the country speaks in three official languages, yet everyone is Swiss. The thing that makes an Italian Swiss *Swiss* is not his happy Latin genes, but his sober national discipline.

To be Swiss, it seems to me, is, above all, to be proud of *not* making mistakes. When that philosophy is applied to making watches or chocolate or prescription drugs or cheese or even wood carvings, it produces some remarkable results.

When it is applied to running a country right for foreign tourists, it's a welcome blessing.

From a visitor's view, it's much more than just making the trains run on time (something the Swiss deserve no more credit for than most other European railroads). It's more than operating one of the best managed and only truly profitable national airline in the world. It's more than offering excellent banking and currency exchange services. There is also a feeling in Switzerland that you will be "looked after" in many other ways, that the innkeepers in literally thousands of small hotels are operating on a tradition of personal service that started here before the Romans came visiting from the south and long before fondue supposedly became a national dish.

In this connection, one of Switzerland's least known but most important national assets in the field of tourism is the large cadré of hotel executives, managers and chefs which has been graduated from a professional school in Lausanne, the famed *École Hôteliere de la Société Suisse des Hôteliers.* It is a national resource of the first importance, a good example of The Swiss Way, a unique school which has a lot to do with assuring that the Swiss hotel business runs right.

The "Lausanne school," as it is usually referred to, has contributed managerial stars not only to Swiss establishments but to great hotels all over the world. Branches of the school are now opening with Swiss government support in both Kenya and Indonesia—which will eventually bring a touch of The Swiss Way to travelers in those countries as well.

Despite its compact size and landlocked position at the heart of Europe, Switzerland is a country of considerable contrasts, from proper Geneva, international capitol of the world, to quaint Gruyere of cheese fame, to Le Locle, birthplace of the horological industry, to glittering St. Moritz, to

Zurich and its financial gnomes. For me, however, the real heart of the country, and perhaps of The Swiss Way, resides in its capitol city, Bern.

Bern is a beautiful non-metropolis, an unpretentious capitol, center of the Bernese Oberland region, gateway to the great mountains, real home of the symbolic bears, a place where, in the evening or on Sunday, people play chess on the painted pavement of the public square, using chessmen as big as small boys which the community provides. Bern is a city of banks and flower markets and chocolate shops and shiny new trolley cars that glide through the old streets as silently as the many Mercedes.

On a clear day, the great snow crowned mass of Jungfrau looks down on all this from a distance and if you're the type who must get to the top of things, there is a fine trip up the mountain via a private railway. The last few thousand feet are through a steep tunnel that will pop your ears and deliver you to a rough and ready summit house where tea is served from stone pots and meals taste good because of where you are.

My Bernese idyll is not a climb, however, but a boat ride on a crystal crescent lake called the Thunsee which stretches long miles from Thun, near Bern, to Interlaken, a town at the feet of the mountains. It is not necessarily a tourist ride; the fare is modest and the white boats go up and down the lake every day year 'round on schedule, calling in at the small port towns along the way, crossing from side to side, taking people where they need to go.

On a fine day, a passenger making a round trip strictly for pleasure will take an unprecedented picture of Switzerland's great mountain range into his mind forever: Jungfrau, Monch and Eiger, the eternal three, rising like stage scenery across the sky, painted by changing light, looming over the end of the lake. The scenic grandeur makes a traveler feel dwarfed, as if the Thunsee boats were toys afloat in a scale-model lake.

Each time I come home from Switzerland, I find I have added some new examples of The Swiss Way to my collection. The last time, it was an incident in a Swiss restaurant up the lake from Geneva. A group of us had just enjoyed an excellent dinner with good wines and the chef-proprietor (quite likely a graduate of the Lausanne school) had been called out of the kitchen to accept our congratulations. He was a hefty, happy man in the traditional costume: white hat and tunic, necker-chief, blue & white checked pants. A conversation began about things Swiss and the subject soon got around to the traditional Minute Man-style preparedness of the country's able-bodied males.

"I understand you must keep your army rifle with you at all times," a member of our party said to the chef.

"True," he said. "Every Swiss male is a soldier at a moment's notice."

My American friend then said, "Okay, I suppose you keep a rifle in your kitchen too?" After which he smiled a little smugly, as if to say that even the Swiss weren't literally perfect.

The chef looked at us all a little incredulously and marched back to his kitchen, signaling a waiter and a couple of busboys to follow.

"I guess that called his bluff," my friend said, laughing with worldly wisdom. But before his private pleasure was complete, the door to the kitchen swung open again and four men marched crisply into the dining room wearing steel army hel-mets that look like the German Wehrmacht and carrying mili-tary rifles at port arms. It was the kitchen staff—chef, assistants and waiter, ready for war.

They came to a halt at the foot of our table and proceeded to rattle smartly through the manual of arms, all of them hardly able to repress their smiles at our surprise.

"You see," said our chef good naturedly at last, "we do not assume that an enemy would not come at meal times!"

That's what I mean about The Swiss Way.

CHAPTER 25
The Enchanted Ferryboat

WE WERE TALKING about Hong Kong one day at lunch—all about the old Crown Colony and the things I like about it—and the New York editor finally said, "Since you have such feelings about this Star Ferry, why don't you write about it? It might make an interesting piece . . ."

It might, indeed, but I never wrote it because when I thought about it, I realized that I really didn't *know* anything about the Star Ferry, not the sort of facts one should have at hand to do a proper magazine article. All I had were memories and feelings.

To put it simply, after many years of friendship and several reunions, I still love the Star Ferry. I think it is, without argument, the most remarkable 4¢ tourist ride in the world, the only form of mass transit which I will gladly take, again and again, purely for pleasure, not really caring in which direction I travel, and always sorry when the journey is ended. For me, it is a sort of enchanted excursion, brief as a ride through the Tunnel of Love, but full of the same feelings of mystery and excitement.

First off, there's the setting. The Star Ferry crosses the world's most beautiful harbor (you'll have to bear with this prejudice) from Hong Kong Island to the tip of the Kowloon peninsula. Imagine taking a boat ride amidst an armada of other craft gathered from all over the world, perhaps a half a hundred major oceangoing ships looming at their moorings, occasionally a giant aircraft carrier or a brace of destroyers, certainly dozens of small boats all scurrying in different directions like many species of water beetles. With them all is the local Chinese flotilla: cargo junks, fishing junks, sampans, Walla-Wallas, tugs, inter-island boats, vehicular ferries, an occasional sightseeing boat, or the old pirate chaser, *Wan Fu,* graceful as a swan among turtles. It is the English Channel on D-day —but in Hong Kong, it is everyday.

The Star Ferry does not skirt this maritime traffic jam, it mingles with it and penetrates it by what seems an combination of rules-of-the-road, navigational agility and divine Buddhist good fortune. The ferry yields now and then to traffic, and is yielded to in turn, but it is always right there in the middle of the hurly-burly, a scrappy participant, not a privileged spectator. As a consequence, a passenger on the Star is afforded an intimate view of all that passes: close enough to read the faces on Australian sailors on the fantail of a warship, or count the children on a sampan, or hear the howl of a chow dog on the deck of a junk.

Not the sort of thing to fall in love with, you say? A short ride, a cheap fare, a busy harbor and a public boat. You say there's a ferry between Manhattan and Staten Island that is famous for all that too? I know. But love is subjective and the Star is *my* ferry.

Perhaps it all goes back to that first time I ever crossed Hong Kong harbor and I stood on the forward deck of the Yaumati car ferry and looked up at Victoria Peak and the booming city which was then beginning to grow up its slopes. I thought it all a fairyland and I was somewhat amazed to be there. I didn't know one ferry from another—there seemed to be many criss-crossing the roadstead—but when my guide pointed and said, "That one's the Star Ferry," he made it sound special and the name seemed familiar, like something I should already know about but didn't. I looked at the small, doubledecked, double-ended boat, white on top, green on the bottom, with only a little more than passing interest. The Star Ferry. Hmm. I thought I would probably ride on it one day.

The fact is, whether he realizes it or not, a visitor will hardly be in Hong Kong for more than a day, or perhaps a few hours, without wanting or needing to cross the harbor. Hong Kong is a city both united and divided by its harbor, and no bridge spans from "island side" to "Kowloon side." You must go via the water—under it, in the new vehicular tunnel, but more likely upon it, in the Star Ferry. It is as inevitable as using the telephone.

The ride takes about 7 minutes in normal weather, as I recall, although if you are a participant it is as hard to time as a kiss. You will have a choice of going first class for about 8¢ or second class for half of that. Tourists, businessmen, snobs, westerners in general, hygiene freaks, and those with an acquired fear of Chinese masses will likely go first class and find their way to seats on the upper deck where there are window-enclosed cabins fore and aft, a somewhat higher shine on the varnished hardwood benches—and still plenty of Chinese. Second class, however, is where the action is and where the view of the harbor is best. It is neither less clean nor much more crowded. Indeed, it is in second class that you may see for yourself how well run a Star ferry is, how gleaming the brass in the engine room, how clean the uniforms of the crew, how precisely coiled the mooring hawsers. The skipper and helmsman have their stations on this lower deck. Here you can feel the throb of the big diesel engines through the teak planking, smell hemp and tar and hear the sound of the engine room bells speaking their universal language of the sea.

But there is more to the appeal of the Star Ferry than nautical paraphernalia, good housekeeping and an interesting route. Perhaps it is the relentless shuttling of this small family of boats, always one or more of them in sight, dawn to dark, sometimes packed with humanity, sometimes almost empty, but always there waiting for you all the same. I became so attached to them that I began to take note of their names: Celestial Star, Day Star, Night Star, Shining Star, Morning Star, Northern Star, Radiant Star, Meridian Star, Solar Star . . . that's all I can remember, although there may be more. Some are no doubt older than others, or different in some ways, yet they all look alike to me, like a litter of pups, friendly and faithful.

Perhaps the true test of my feelings about the ferry came some years ago when I took Karen to Hong Kong for her first visit. I'm sure I had filled my new bride's head with many tall tales and well-intentioned exaggerations about this place which has always fascinated me so. I suppose it was all because I hoped she would feel the same way I did about it. At any rate, I was anxious that all would go well, that her first impressions would be filled with the same magic that I felt, that we would love the place together.

First, of course, there was the landing at Kai Tak, that seemingly precarious runway which juts into the harbor, then the taxi ride through the swarming streets to the hotel, then a first look from the balcony across to the distant mountains called the

Seven Dragons of Kowloon.

Then I said, "See down there? Those little boats?"

It was getting dark, but Karen followed my eye to the pier just below.

"It's the Star Ferry, isn't it?" she said.

I nodded and said, "Let's go!" Our bags stood unopened. We hadn't even washed our faces or thought about finding the bar. We looked at each other and laughed at what we were going to do.

Across the street we went and through the turnstiles and down the length of the pier, all lined and lighted with watch and camera ads, and there, waiting, ramps lowered, engines rumbling softly, was—which Star? It didn't matter. We stepped aboard and went forward and each of us leaned out a window at the bow.

It was almost dark now, a lovely spring evening, one of those nights when the lights of this many-splendored place looked like billions of individual stars. They reflected on the rippling black water, multi-colored, liquid, as if the rainbow content of the neon tubes themselves had spilled out to float on the surface with us.

A bell rang in the distance and the ramps rattled up and the boat groaned like a giant bow being scraped against the pilings as it moved, all trembling now, headed, perpetually, for the other side. Not far away, a companion Star was arriving, angling toward our vacated slip, lights ablaze, passengers crowding toward the gangways. It passed behind us and left only anticipation ahead.

◆   ◆   ◆

I don't know how many people use the Star Ferry each day or each year, or how many feet long or wide the boats are, or who owns the company which operates them, or on what day and date the service began, or why the boats are named for stars, or how many there are, or how the captains are trained, or if any ferry has ever foundered, or what the horsepower of the engines may be, or how many life rafts there are for how many passengers, or what percentage of people go first class, or who keeps the boats so clean, or what happens in a typhoon— as I say, I don't have any of the necessary facts or anecdotes with which to write an article about the Star Ferry.

All I know is, if you ever arrive in Hong Kong with someone you love, find Celestial Star or any of her sisters and go for a quick round trip across the harbor. It will take less than half an hour, but you will remember it as long as you live.